easy does it

entertaining

Patty Roper

by patty roper

For two Elizabeths who have blessed my life—
my mother, Evelyn Elizabeth Slay, and
my daughter, Marie Elizabeth Roper

introduction

I love entertaining and making people feel special. I enjoy planning and organizing ideas, creating special presentations, preparing menus and decorations, and orchestrating overall events. From an intimate luncheon or tea party with a few special friends to a formal dinner party for many to a holiday gathering with all the family, entertaining is a way of sharing the milestones of life with others through our gracious hospitality. In celebrating these special times, memories are created, traditions are founded, and heritage is formed. In the South, we are our heritage. We share our past experiences with the present generation, and they in turn pass this heritage on to the future generation. Our children grow up tasting delicious family recipes served on heirloom china and silver and hearing memorable stories of relatives and friends. The recipes in this book are favorites shared by my heritage of family and friends.

Memories and traditions take time. Time is truly one of the most valuable gifts we can share with others, and it is certainly a premium in our fast-paced society. For this reason, we need easy solutions that are beautiful as well as efficient. We need simple recipes that are delicious and practical party suggestions that become beautiful memories.

This book is designed to help you enter each season with fresh ideas and easy-to-prepare menus to make your celebrations and special occasions full of ease and enjoyment. It is my desire for you not only to love entertaining but also to make it an Easy Does It way of life to share with friends and family.

Patty Roper

acknowledgments

Thank you to God for His sovereign guidance throughout this project and my life.

Thank you to:

My husband, Richard, for encouragement and confidence

My mother, Evelyn Slay, for a heritage of recipes for food and life

My daughter, Beth, for sharing life with me in any endeavor

Lena Causey for cooking, testing, and sharing recipes

Mary Graves for sharing her love of nature and flowers and her lovely home with me

Gail Collins, Linn Harris, Maggi Lampton, Patty Mitchell, and Deedee Sheely for sharing their homes and gardens

Sarabeth Atkins for cooking and testing recipes

Linda Rochelle for preparing food and sharing recipes

The many friends and family members who shared recipes, ideas, and encouragement

Greg Campbell, my photographer and friend, for capturing my ideas with beauty

Kelli Bozeman for invaluable and diligent editing

Tempy Segrest for photographing and for her artistic design talent that gives life to these pages

Greg Campbell and Tempy Segrest, Photographers
Kelli Bozeman, Editor
Tempy Segrest, Art Director

ISBN 0-9654769-4-4

First Edition, 2004
0 1 2 3 4 5 6 7 8 9 10

Printed in Mexico

contents

Spring

Exuberant displays of buds and flowers
promise fruit, while bulbs offer an impressionistic
palette of fragrance and beauty that is
here today, gone tomorrow.
It happens overnight, and suddenly
with daybreak everything is new.
It is full of sunlight, enhancing the colors
of vitality and energy in the landscape of our lives.
God is in His heaven, and His love abounds.

camellia *brunch*

BAKED CHILI RELLEÑOS

6 thin slices bread
Butter
2 cups cheddar cheese, shredded
2 cups Monterey Jack cheese, shredded
1 (4-ounce) can minced green chilies
6 eggs
2 cups milk
½ teaspoon salt
¼ teaspoon paprika
½ teaspoon pepper
1 teaspoon oregano
¼ teaspoon dry mustard
Sour cream and cilantro for garnish

Cut crusts off bread slices. Butter bread, and place buttered side down in a 7 x 11 x 2-inch baking dish. Sprinkle cheddar cheese evenly over bread. Add Monterey Jack cheese and green chilies. In a bowl, beat eggs, then add milk and seasonings. Pour egg mixture over cheeses and chilies. Cover with foil; refrigerate for 4 hours or overnight. Preheat oven to 325 degrees. Bake uncovered for about 50 minutes or until top browns. Let stand for 10 minutes before serving. Cut into squares; garnish with a dollop of sour cream and a sprig of cilantro. Yield: 8-10 servings.

Brunches are excellent ways to entertain. A mid-morning gathering just seems to add a relaxing element to the week. Much of the food can be prepared in advance, and an outside setting is usually refreshing. Buffet service often works well, giving the host and hostess more time to visit with the guests.

Set up small tables on porches, decks, and patios. Be sure to have extra tea and coffee for lingering guests.

PUMPKIN MUFFINS
WITH ORANGE PECAN BUTTER

½ cup butter
1 cup sugar
2 eggs
1 cup pumpkin
3 cups all-purpose flour
4 teaspoons baking powder
½ teaspoon cinnamon
½ teaspoon ground cloves
½ teaspoon ginger
½ teaspoon nutmeg
1 teaspoon salt
1¼ cups milk

Preheat oven to 400 degrees. Grease miniature muffin tins. Cream butter and sugar; beat in eggs and pumpkin. Sift together flour, baking powder, spices, and salt. Add dry ingredients and milk to pumpkin mixture alternately by hand, mixing just until blended. Do not overmix. Spoon into prepared tins, filling ¾ full. Bake for about 12-15 minutes or until lightly browned. Serve with Orange Pecan Butter. Yield: 4 dozen miniature or 2 dozen standard muffins.

ORANGE PECAN BUTTER:
½ cup pecans, chopped
1 cup butter, softened
1½ tablespoons orange rind, grated
Orange rind strips and toasted pecans for garnish

Bake pecans in a shallow pan at 350 degrees, stirring occasionally, for 5-10 minutes until toasted. Beat butter on medium speed with a mixer until creamy. Add pecans and grated orange rind, beating until blended. Chill for up to 2 days; let stand at room temperature to soften before serving. Place in a serving bowl; garnish with orange strips and pecans. Yield: 1½ cups.

CHEDDAR CHEESE BISCUITS WITH HAM

2 cups plus 2 tablespoons all-purpose flour
4 teaspoons baking powder
½ teaspoon salt
6 tablespoons cold butter, cubed
½ cup sharp cheddar cheese, grated
¾ cup buttermilk
6 to 8 slices cooked ham

Preheat oven to 425 degrees. Butter a baking sheet, and set aside. In the bowl of a food processor, combine flour, baking powder, and salt, and process briefly to combine. Add butter and cheese, and process until the mixture resembles coarse meal. Pour in buttermilk, then process until dough comes together, about 15 seconds. Turn dough onto a floured board, and allow to rest for 5 minutes. Knead 3 times only, then roll out to a ½-inch thickness. Cut into desired shapes. Place on a baking sheet, and bake for 10-15 minutes or until puffed and golden. Slice each biscuit in half, butter, and insert a piece of cooked ham. Yield: 12-16.

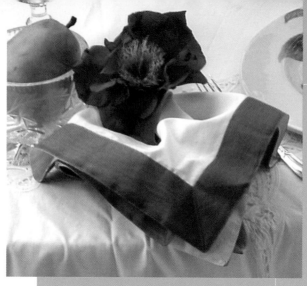

COLORFUL NAPKINS

Add color to basic napkins by painting the edges with fabric paint to coordinate with table décor.

You will need:
White fabric napkins
Fabric paint
Sponge brush

On each napkin, paint a border of desired width or width of hem with fabric paint. Follow directions on fabric paint to set paint before washing.

easy does it

HONEY-YOGURT SAUCE ON FRUIT

¾ cup vanilla yogurt
2 tablespoons honey
Fresh seasonal fruit

Mix; store in refrigerator until ready to serve. (You may adjust the amount of honey to taste.) Serve over fresh seasonal fruit.

Beautiful summer blooms are pretty touches when placed on napkins or under napkin rings. Napkins should be placed on serving plates or to the left of forks.

RASPBERRY CREAM CHEESE COFFEE CAKE

2¼ cups all-purpose flour
1 cup sugar, divided
¾ cup butter
½ teaspoon baking powder
½ teaspoon baking soda
¼ teaspoon salt
¾ cup sour cream
1 teaspoon almond extract
2 eggs
1 (8-ounce) package cream cheese, softened
½ cup raspberry preserves
½ cup sliced almonds
Fresh raspberries and almonds for garnish

Preheat oven to 350 degrees. Grease and flour bottom and sides of a 9- or 10-inch springform pan. In a large bowl, combine flour and ¾ cup sugar. Using a pastry blender or fork, cut in butter until mixture resembles coarse crumbs. Reserve 1 cup of crumb mixture. To remaining crumb mixture, add baking powder, baking soda, salt, sour cream, almond extract, and 1 egg; blend well. Spread batter over the bottom and 2 inches up the sides of the greased and floured pan. (Batter should be about ¼ inch thick on the sides.) In a small bowl, combine cream cheese, ¼ cup sugar, and 1 egg; blend well. Pour into batter-lined pan. Carefully spoon preserves evenly over cream cheese mixture. In a small bowl, combine reserved crumb mixture and almonds. Sprinkle over preserves. Bake for 45-55 minutes or until cream cheese filling is set and crust is golden brown. Cool 15 minutes, then remove the sides of the pan. Garnish with fresh raspberries and almond slices. Serve warm or cool, cut into wedges. Store in the refrigerator. Yield: 16 servings.

Have a serve-yourself juice bar as guests arrive.
Serve several different juices in clear glass pitchers
to reveal the types of juice and to create a colorful display.
Be sure to add fresh fruit and lots of mint to each pitcher.
Ice cubes made with frozen juice will not dilute the juice.
Freeze grapes or fresh flowers in ice cubes, or freeze
whole lemons, limes, or kumquats to add to the juice pitchers.
Serve the juice in pretty stemmed goblets with cocktail napkins.

POSY COOKIES

Flowers are a must when entertaining, but these pretty posies are actually delicious three-dimensional cookies. Serve them with coffee or tea, or present them as favors in cellophane bags with bows.

BUTTER SUGAR COOKIES:
2 cups butter, softened
1 cup sugar
1 egg
1 teaspoon vanilla
4½ cups all-purpose flour, sifted

Preheat oven to 375 degrees. Cream butter and sugar; add egg and vanilla. Gradually add flour. Shape into 4 balls; cover and refrigerate for 1 hour. Remove, and roll out ⅛ to ¼ inch thick. Use different cookie cutter combinations (heart, star, and flower), and layer and fold shapes. Bake for 6-9 minutes or until light golden on the edges. Cool cookies on a wire rack, and paint with Egg White Wash. Yield: about 2 dozen.

EGG WHITE WASH:
2 egg whites
Paste food coloring
Few drops water

Divide egg whites into a few small bowls. Add a small amount of food coloring and a few drops of water to each bowl. Paint cookies, and allow to dry before painting stamens or veins. Return cookies to oven for about 1 minute to set the egg white.

PEDESTAL CAKE STANDS

These cake stands will add a special touch to any dessert sideboard.

You will need:
Candlestick with a sturdy base,
*   no taller than 14 inches (wood,*
*   plastic, or ceramic)*
Plastic banquet plate
Electric drill, metal screws,
*   and screwdriver*
Multipurpose clear-drying cement
Glass cake dome
Glass cleaner, primer, and clear glaze
Gold leaf adhesive size and
*   gold leaf sheets*

Secure banquet plate to candlestick base with screw or cement. To add gold to glass dome, clean and prime area. Add gold leaf according to package directions. Seal with clear glaze.

easy does it

birthday *tea* for a friend

CHICKEN CRESCENTS

1 (13-ounce) can fully cooked
chunk chicken breast in water,
drained
½ (8-ounce) container cream
cheese with chives
2½ tablespoons melted butter,
divided
½ can cream of chicken soup
¼ teaspoon salt
¼ teaspoon white pepper
2 cans crescent rolls
1 sleeve saltine crackers,
crumbled

Preheat oven to 350 degrees. Combine chicken, cream cheese, 1½ tablespoons melted butter, soup, salt, and pepper. Roll out crescent rolls, and place 1 tablespoon of chicken filling on each triangle. Pinch edges closed. Place on a baking pan sprayed with non-stick cooking spray, and brush crescents with remaining melted butter; sprinkle cracker crumbs on top. Bake for about 10 minutes. Yield: 16.

Blue and white china is always pretty and gives an Old World feeling.
Flow blue and Blue Willow mix beautifully, and antique
and new pieces blend nicely for an eclectic appeal.

Yellow flowers will bring the blue and white color scheme to life.

Louisiana irises, alstroemeria, tulips, and daffodils are the essence of a spring welcome. What could be more memorable than a birthday among a sea of yellow irises?

DATE AND WALNUT SANDWICHES

8 large slices raisin bread
3 tablespoons cream cheese, softened
1 tablespoon honey
1 teaspoon ground cinnamon
⅓ cup walnuts, finely chopped
½ cup dates, chopped

Spread cream cheese on all bread slices. Spread honey on 4 slices, and sprinkle with cinnamon. Scatter walnuts and chopped dates on the honey side. Place remaining slices on top. Remove crusts, and slice into 3 fingers per sandwich. Yield: 12.

TOMATO SANDWICH ROUNDS

1 loaf white bread
½ cup mayonnaise
¼ teaspoon Tabasco sauce
Lemon pepper, salt, and white pepper to taste
4 homegrown tomatoes, sliced
Fresh basil
Real bacon bits

Cut a round from each slice of bread with a biscuit cutter. Mix mayonnaise, Tabasco, lemon pepper, salt, and pepper. Spread each bread round with the mayonnaise mixture, top with a tomato slice, and sprinkle with basil and bacon bits. Yield: 24.

Old damask linens never go out of style, and tablecloths do not always have to exactly fit the table. Layering several cloths will give a fresh look. Matelassé bedspreads make wonderful table coverings and are available in generous sizes. The thickness of the fabric adds nice texture, and they are easily cleaned and need little or no ironing.

POSY BAGS

Create decorations for your party and favors for your guests from coordinating fabrics.

You will need:

Fabric to go with your tablescape
Heavy-duty Ziploc freezer bags
Cords or ribbons

Stitch the fabric to create a bag about 6 x 9 inches. Place the freezer bag inside to create a plastic lining. Fold in the top inch of fabric, then stitch around this top hem, making sure that the top of the freezer bag is inserted into the folded-down edge before sewing. Add a handle about 13 inches long, made from fabric, ribbon, or cord. Fill with a small amount of water and a posy arrangement, and hang or tie on the backs of chairs.

easy does it

CUCUMBER SANDWICHES

1 stick butter, softened
1 (8-ounce) package cream cheese
1 tablespoon lemon juice
½ teaspoon salt
½ teaspoon white pepper
1 cucumber, peeled
16 thin slices white bread

Combine butter, cream cheese, and lemon juice. Season with salt and pepper. Set aside. Slice cucumber very thinly. Flatten bread, and spread each piece with butter spread. Layer cucumbers on one side of bread, and top with another piece. Remove crusts, and cut into small sandwiches. Yield: 16.

LEMON SCONES

2 cups all-purpose flour
½ teaspoon salt
4 tablespoons sugar
1 tablespoon baking powder
3½ tablespoons butter, softened
1 (8-ounce) container lemon yogurt
2 egg yolks
2 teaspoons lemon zest
3 tablespoons heavy cream
Melted butter
Sugar for sprinkling

Preheat oven to 425 degrees. Mix together flour, salt, sugar, and baking powder. Using a pastry blender, cut in butter until mixture resembles coarse crumbs. Stir together lemon yogurt, egg yolks, and lemon zest. Add to flour mixture, and stir lightly with fork. Add cream, 1 tablespoon at a time, until dough clumps together. Set dough on a lightly floured surface, and knead 3 or 4 times until dough holds together. Roll to about ¾ inch thick, and cut out shapes with a cookie cutter. Place about 1 inch apart on an ungreased cookie sheet. Brush with melted butter, and sprinkle with sugar. Bake for 8 minutes. Yield: about 2 dozen.

BLACKBERRY OR MARION BERRY JAM

4 cups blackberries or Marion berries, crushed
1½ cups sugar
1 (1.59-ounce) pouch Fruit Jell freezer jam pectin

Combine berries and sugar in a medium bowl, and let stand 15 minutes. Gradually stir Fruit Jell into the fruit mixture. Stir for 3 minutes, and let stand for 5 minutes. Ladle into freezer containers, leaving ½ inch of room at top. Seal, and freeze. Jam will keep in freezer for 1 year or in refrigerator for up to 3 weeks. Yield: about five 8-ounce containers.

CITRUS FRUIT CUPS WITH ORANGE-MINT DRESSING

2 cups orange sections
2 cups grapefruit sections
1 cup grapes
1 cup kiwis, sliced
1 cup mandarin oranges

Toss together all ingredients. Drizzle with Orange-Mint Dressing just before serving. Yield: 8 cups.

ORANGE-MINT DRESSING:
½ cup sugar
⅓ cup orange juice
⅓ cup lemon juice
⅛ teaspoon peppermint extract

Combine all ingredients, mixing well. Yield: 1 cup.

Scones are light, tender biscuits served warm with butter, jam, lemon curd, or cream. They may be seasoned with fruits, nuts, herbs, or spices.

CINNAMON MADELEINES

2 eggs, beaten
1 cup sugar
1 cup all-purpose flour
¾ cup butter, melted and cooled
½ teaspoon cinnamon
½ teaspoon almond extract
Confectioner's sugar for sprinkling

Preheat oven to 350 degrees. Spray molds with non-stick cooking spray, or lightly coat with vegetable oil. In a double boiler, heat eggs and sugar until lukewarm, stirring constantly. Remove from heat, and beat until batter thickens, incorporating as much air as possible. Once cool, gradually stir in flour. Then add butter, cinnamon, and almond extract. Fill molds ⅔ full of batter, but do not spread it out. Bake until brown, about 15 minutes. (Tops will spring back when pressed lightly.) Cool in pan for 1 minute, then turn madeleines out on a rack to cool completely. Sprinkle with confectioner's sugar. Yield: about 1½-2 dozen.

ITALIAN CREAM CAKE

1 stick margarine
½ cup shortening
2 cups sugar
5 eggs, separated
1 teaspoon baking soda
1 cup buttermilk
2 cups all-purpose flour, sifted
1 teaspoon salt
1 can flaked coconut
1 cup pecans, chopped
1 teaspoon vanilla

Preheat oven to 325 degrees. Grease and flour three 9-inch square cake pans. Cream margarine, shortening, and sugar. Beat well, and add egg yolks, 1 at a time, beating for 1 minute after each addition. Mix soda and buttermilk; add alternately with flour and salt to egg yolk mixture. Add coconut, pecans, and vanilla. Beat egg whites until stiff, and fold into batter. Pour into pans. Bake for 30 minutes. Remove to wire racks to cool, and frost with Cream Cheese Frosting. Yield: 20 servings.

CREAM CHEESE FROSTING:

1 (8-ounce) package cream cheese, softened
½ cup margarine, softened
1 teaspoon vanilla
1 box confectioner's sugar, sifted
1 cup pecans, chopped
½ cup canned flaked coconut

Beat cream cheese and margarine until light and fluffy. Add vanilla and sugar. Beat until smooth. Stir in pecans and coconut. Spread between layers, and frost cake.

Afternoon tea, usually served
from 3 to 5 p.m., is perfect
for a birthday celebration.
Light fare is followed by an extravagant cake!

PRESENT BIRTHDAY CAKES

Wrap your most delicious desserts by tying them with rolled fondant bows. Place them on squares of glass attached to the tops of candlesticks with floral clay. After square cakes are prepared, follow these easy instructions for creating fondant bows.

You will need:
1 package prepared rolled fondant
Paste food coloring
Rolling pin
Scissors
Sharp knife
2 to 3 squares almond bark, melted
Pastry bag with a small tip, or small plastic bag

Knead food coloring into prepared rolled fondant icing to create desired color. Roll out fondant on waxed paper, and cut into strips about ¼ inch wide. Cut bow loop strips about 7 inches long, and loop around foil to hold each individual loop. For streamers, cut the ends in V's or slants. Position the streamers on crumpled foil to give them dimension. Make curls by wrapping fondant strips around a pencil. Allow bow loops and streamers to dry for about 2 days. When dry and hardened, roll out additional fondant for cross pieces, and place the cross ribbons on each cake from side to side. "Glue" loops to set bow, streamers, and curls in desired positions by applying melted almond bark with a pastry bag or a small plastic bag with a hole cut in the corner.

easy does it

LEMON ICEBOX CAKE

1 box lemon supreme cake mix
½ cup oil
1 cup water
3 eggs

Preheat oven to 350 degrees. Combine all ingredients, and beat for 2 minutes. Grease three 8-inch square cake pans. Pour batter into pans, and bake for 18-20 minutes. Allow to cool. Stack cake layers, spreading Filling between layers. Top with Icing.

FILLING:
2 cans sweetened condensed milk
¾ cup fresh-squeezed lemon juice

Mix together. Reserve ½ cup of mixture for Icing.

ICING:
½ cup reserved Filling
1 (8-ounce) container whipped topping

Mix together reserved Filling and whipped topping, and frost cake. Refrigerate for 1 day before serving.

Sharing tea or coffee signifies
trust and friendship.
The drink of choice at a tea
may be either hot or cold.
It may even be a
flavored coffee or
hot chocolate.

YELLOW CAKE

1 box yellow cake mix
1 cup water
½ cup oil
1 teaspoon vanilla
4 eggs

Preheat oven to 350 degrees. Grease two 9-inch or three 8-inch square cake pans. Blend dry cake mix, water, oil, vanilla, and eggs in a large bowl. Beat on medium speed for 2 minutes. Pour into pans. Bake for 20-23 minutes. Frost with Easy Caramel or Chocolate Icing.

EASY CARAMEL ICING:
½ cup butter
1 cup light brown sugar, firmly packed
⅓ cup evaporated milk
2 cups confectioner's sugar
1 teaspoon vanilla

Melt butter in a medium saucepan. Add brown sugar, and bring to a boil, stirring for 1 minute. Remove saucepan from heat, and add evaporated milk. Return to low heat, then bring to a boil. Remove from heat, and cool slightly or to 110 degrees on candy thermometer. Beat in confectioner's sugar with a wooden spoon or portable electric mixer until frosting is thick. If too thin, add a little more confectioner's sugar. Add vanilla. Place saucepan in a bowl of ice water, and beat until frosting reaches spreading consistency. Make 2 recipes for a 3-layer cake, but do not double recipe.

EASY CHOCOLATE ICING:
6 ounces vanilla-flavored almond bark
1 (16-ounce) can milk chocolate frosting
1 teaspoon vanilla

Melt almond bark in a microwave-safe bowl at 1-minute intervals on low for about 3 minutes. Stir in canned frosting and vanilla. Make 2 recipes for a 3-layer cake, but do not double recipe.

ICED INDIAN TEA

Juice of 4 lemons
5 regular-size tea bags
1 cup boiling water
1 tablespoon almond flavoring
1 tablespoon vanilla
4 cups water
1½ cups sugar
1 quart ginger ale

Combine lemon juice, tea bags, and 1 cup boiling water. Cover, and let stand for 20 minutes. Add next 4 ingredients. Chill. Add ginger ale just before serving. Yield: about 1 gallon.

Add individual vases to each
place setting. A small nametag
may be attached to each
vase as a placecard.
Or in keeping with the birthday theme,
wrap a small present with a favor
inside to use as a placecard.
Any individual item will
add a special touch.

easter *celebration*

Shape cookies like decorated eggs, and cut biscuits in shapes of bunnies or chicks. Fashion a carrot cake into an Easter bonnet. Decorate a cream cheese spread like a smiling, winking bunny by adding colorful vegetables.

HAM AND SWISS CHEESE ROLLS

1 (16-ounce) canned ham
2 tablespoons Grey Poupon mustard
2 tablespoons brown sugar
2 packages Sister Schubert's Parker House rolls
½ stick butter, softened
2 tablespoons Dijon mustard
2 tablespoons poppy seeds
1 (16-slice) package Swiss cheese

Preheat oven to 275 degrees. Spread canned ham with Grey Poupon mustard and brown sugar. Wrap in foil, and bake for 1 hour. Allow ham to cool. Chop ham into small pieces, and set aside.

Without separating packages of rolls, slice horizontally with a sharp knife. Replace the top of one roll so that all tops will be easier to replace later. Spread bottoms and tops of rolls with a mixture of butter, Dijon mustard, and poppy seeds. Sprinkle with chopped ham, then top with Swiss cheese slices. Replace tops of rolls, and separate rolls with a sharp knife. Bake in pan according to package directions and serve immediately, or freeze in original package before baking. Yield: about 32 rolls.

CHERRY TOMATO CUPS

1 (5-ounce) container herbed goat cheese
16 to 20 cherry tomatoes
2 tablespoons chives, snipped

Let cheese stand at room temperature about 20 minutes to soften. Slice off bottoms of tomatoes so they are flat. Cut large slices from stem ends, and hollow with melon baller. Drain upside down on paper towels. Spoon cheese into tomatoes, mounding slightly. Sprinkle with chives. May be chilled, covered, for 24 hours. Yield: 16-20.

STUFFED NEW POTATOES

15 small new potatoes, unpeeled
⅓ cup ricotta cheese
⅓ cup cream cheese
1 tablespoon onion, minced
1 tablespoon Dijon mustard
½ teaspoon vinegar
Paprika to taste
Fresh parsley sprigs for garnish

Place potatoes in a vegetable steamer over boiling water. Cover, and steam for 15-20 minutes or until tender. Remove from steamer, and let cool. Cut each potato in half. Combine ricotta, cream cheese, onion, mustard, and vinegar. Spoon mixture onto each potato half. Sprinkle with paprika, and garnish with a small sprig of parsley. Yield: about 30.

Serve refreshments on a large Easter basket table.
Cover the top of a skirted table with green sheet moss or grass sod.
Attach a pussy willow basket handle with bouquet-holder clamps.
Wire the pussy willow in the center to form a curved handle.
Place spring flowers in the vases
of the bouquet clamps, and add ribbons.
Decorate with natural materials, bunnies, and chicks.
Serve cookies and cupcakes on paper liners.

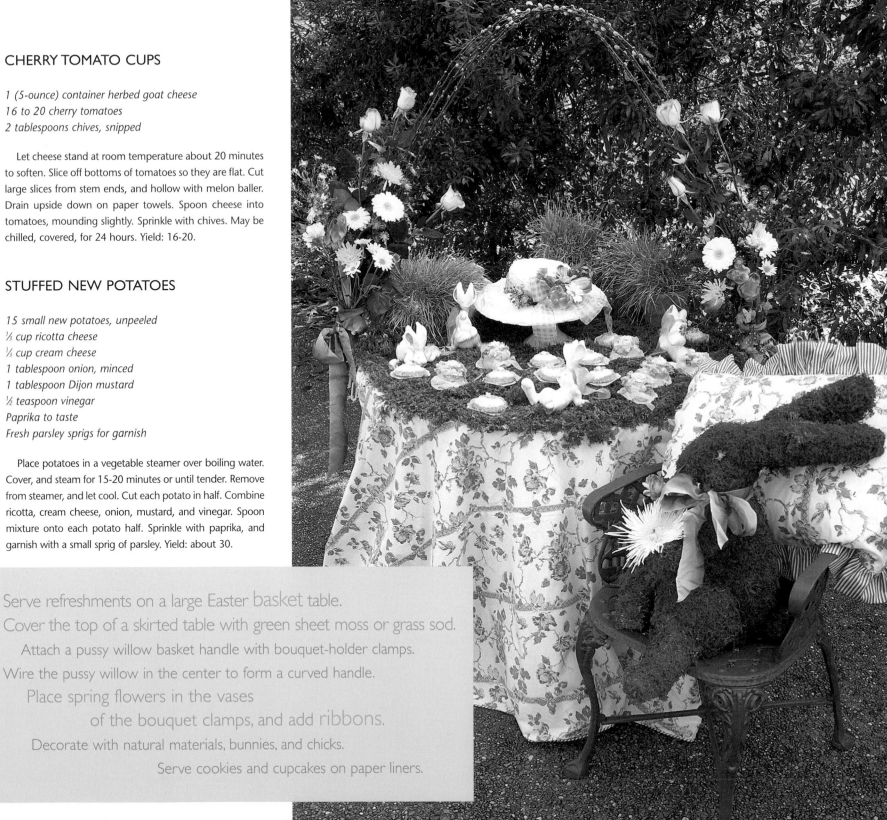

SESAME BISCUITS

1¾ cups all-purpose flour
2 teaspoons baking powder
½ teaspoon salt
⅓ cup vegetable shortening
½ cup plain yogurt
½ cup milk
2 tablespoons butter, melted
Sesame seeds

Preheat oven to 450 degrees. Grease baking sheets. Combine flour, baking powder, and salt in a mixing bowl. Using a pastry blender, cut shortening into flour mixture until it resembles peas. Blend in yogurt and milk. Pat dough down to a ½-inch thickness on a well-floured surface. Cut out with floured cutters. Place on a baking sheet. Brush tops with melted butter, and sprinkle with sesame seeds. Bake for 12 minutes, then place under the broiler for a few minutes to brown. Yield: about 16.

BUNNY CREAM CHEESE SPREAD

2 (8-ounce) packages cream cheese, softened
2 teaspoons caraway seed
2 teaspoons dried basil leaves
2 teaspoons dried dill
2 teaspoons dried chives
½ teaspoon garlic salt
Lemon pepper to taste
1 can pasteurized processed cheese spread
3 tablespoons yellow bell pepper, chopped
3 tablespoons red bell pepper, chopped
Fresh chives
Black olives
Leaf lettuce for garnish

Cut bunny head pattern from parchment paper as a guide. Place on a platter. In a medium bowl, beat cream cheese until fluffy. Add caraway seed, basil, dill, chives, garlic salt, and lemon pepper; beat until well-blended. Spread cream cheese mixture on bunny head pattern.

Outline bunny with canned cheese spread. Fill in bow tie with yellow bell pepper and ears with red bell pepper. Make nose and mouth with red bell pepper and whiskers with chives. Use half of a black olive for the open eye, and cut black olives into slivers to make winking eye and lashes. Garnish with leaf lettuce. Serve with sesame biscuits or crackers. Yield: 20-30 servings.

TINY ORANGE MUFFINS WITH CRANBERRY CHUTNEY AND TURKEY

1 teaspoon baking soda
1 cup buttermilk
½ cup butter
1 cup sugar
2 eggs, slightly beaten
Zest of 2 oranges
2 cups all-purpose flour
1 small jar cranberry chutney
Several thin slices deli-style turkey

Preheat oven to 375 degrees. Grease miniature muffin tins. Dissolve baking soda in buttermilk. Cream butter and sugar; add eggs and orange zest, and mix well. Stir in flour and buttermilk mixture alternately. Mix well. Fill muffin tins ⅔ full, and bake for 8 minutes. While muffins are baking, make Orange Syrup. Remove muffins from tins, and dip tops into Orange Syrup. Let dry for 1 hour. Slice muffins, spread with cranberry chutney, and stuff with turkey. Yield: about 48.

ORANGE SYRUP:
½ cup sugar
½ cup orange juice

Mix sugar and orange juice; bring to a boil, and heat until thickened, about 3-5 minutes.

"FABERGÉ" EGG MADE OF FLOWERS

This flower-covered egg makes a spectacular centerpiece.

You will need:
2 blocks floral foam
3 bunches lime Kermit button mums
Roses, ivy leaves, and hypericum berries

Glue two blocks of foam together, and wet. Cut into an egg shape, and cover with lime mums. Place on a bed of leaves on a pedestal or plate. Place a few leaves, roses, and berries on top. This egg will stay fresh for several days and even longer if refrigerated between displays.

easy does it

An egg hunt is fun for all ages, with the appropriate favors in plastic eggs.

FRESH FRUIT ON SKEWERS

Cantaloupe, cut into chunks
Pineapple, cut into chunks
Green and red seedless grapes
Strawberries
Wood skewers
Cantaloupe half for base

Thread fruit onto skewers; insert into cantaloupe half.

MELTING MOMENT EGG COOKIES

COOKIES:
1 cup butter
⅓ cup confectioner's sugar
⅔ cup cornstarch
1 cup flour

Preheat oven to 350 degrees. Cream butter and sugar. Sift together cornstarch and flour. Add cornstarch and flour to butter and sugar, and blend well. Shape dough by teaspoonfuls into egg shapes, and place on an ungreased cookie sheet about 1 inch apart. Bake for about 10 minutes. Do not brown. Cookies should be white and baked to the "melt-in-your-mouth" point, not crisp. Carefully remove cookies from cookie sheet, and cool. Cookies will be very fragile. Yield: about 18-20.

FROSTING:
3 tablespoons lemon juice
3 cups confectioner's sugar
⅓ cup butter, softened
Red and green food coloring

Combine first 3 ingredients, and beat until creamy. Divide into 2 portions. Use half to ice egg cookies. Divide remaining half into 2 portions, and tint half pink and half light green. Decorate by piping onto egg cookies with pastry bag.

CARROT CAKE HAT

4 eggs
2 cups carrots, finely grated
1½ cups oil
1 teaspoon vanilla
2 cups sugar
2 cups self-rising flour, sifted
2 teaspoons cinnamon
½ teaspoon ginger

Preheat oven to 350 degrees. Mix together eggs, carrots, and oil. Add vanilla, sugar, flour, cinnamon, and ginger. If mixture is too dry, add a few drops more oil. Pour into 2 greased and floured 8-inch round cake pans. Bake for about 30 minutes or until toothpick comes out clean. Cool before icing. Use 2-layer cake for crown of hat; make another half recipe for rim of hat, and bake in a 14-inch pizza pan.

To assemble hat, place 14-inch cake on a large platter, and frost with Icing. Frost 2-layer cake, and place as crown on brim. Tie ribbon around crown of hat, and decorate with flowers. Yield: 12-16 servings.

ICING:
1 stick butter, softened
1 (8-ounce) package cream cheese, softened
1 (16-ounce) box confectioner's sugar
1 teaspoon vanilla

Cream butter and cream cheese. Add confectioner's sugar, and mix well. Add vanilla, and beat well.

EGG GARLAND

Make a beautiful garland of pastel eggs with soft bows and small dried flowers to trail down your table or hang from a mantel or mirror.

You will need:
12 to 16 Marbleized Eggs (see page 20)
4 yards (¼-inch) ivory ribbon
10 yards (2-inch) ivory organza ribbon
Large crewel sewing needle
Quick Grab clear glue
Dried rosebuds and greenery

Thread eggs of various colors on ¼-inch ribbon using crewel needle. Tie organza bows between each egg, and glue dried material between eggs. Tie bows and streamers on each end.

easy does it

MARBLEIZED EGGS

These beautiful handpainted eggs are very easy to paint and look great tucked into grass in pots and houseplants.

You will need:
Raw eggs
Pin
Pastel latex paints
Paintbrush
Sponge
Clear acrylic spray sealer

Pierce both ends of each raw egg with a pin, and blow out the contents. Wash, then drain and dry. Paint each egg the desired color, and allow to dry. To marbleize the eggs, place a small amount of paint that is the color of the egg and a small amount of cream-colored paint on a paper. Do not mix the paints initially. Use a sponge to apply a little of each color together on the painted egg. When egg is dry, spray with clear acrylic spray sealer.

EGGSHELL VASES

Use eggshells as vases to continue the Easter theme. Several in a line on a table or three in a grouping look especially nice.

You will need:
Marbleized Eggs
Small scissors
Fresh flowers
Egg cups

Using small scissors, crack off a small opening in each Marbleized Egg; place a tiny bouquet inside. Egg cups serve as bases for these miniature eggshell vases.

You may also purchase large ostrich and emu eggs with small drilled holes in the tops. Simply place each egg on a stand or candlestick to hold it upright, fill it with water, then add a single flower or several stems for a special look.

easy does it

FLOWER CUPCAKES

CUPCAKES:
1 box white cake mix
1 teaspoon vanilla
1 teaspoon almond extract
1 teaspoon butter flavoring

Follow package directions to make cake, using egg whites only. Before baking, add vanilla, almond extract, and butter flavoring. Bake according to package directions in a muffin tin, using cupcake liners. Cool, and frost with Buttercream Icing. Yield: 24.

BUTTERCREAM ICING:
1 cup vegetable shortening
1 teaspoon vanilla
1 teaspoon almond extract
1 teaspoon butter flavoring
Pinch salt
1 pound confectioner's sugar
½ to 1 cup whole milk

In a large mixing bowl using an electric mixer, blend shortening, flavorings, and salt. Slowly add confectioner's sugar. Mixture will become very stiff. Add ½ cup milk. Add more milk, 1 tablespoon at a time, until icing is smooth and silky. It should be easy to spread. Spread on cupcakes. For flowers and foliage piped directly onto cupcakes, add more confectioner's sugar to stiffen texture. For roses and more intricate flowers, add small amounts of cornstarch to icing, and make flowers separately on a rose nail. Let dry on waxed paper. These can be made in advance and stored in a cookie tin for several days.

Fashion a wire bunny from small-gauge chicken wire, and glue sheet moss to the wire.

Use dried flowers for eyes, and don't forget a bow on his neck and a bouquet in his arms.

Wheat grass containers are great for displaying eggs on the dining table, buffet, or coffee table.
To grow wheat grass in containers, start a few weeks before Easter by placing potting soil in a container or clay pot.
Scatter wheat seeds on the surface of the soil, and cover with a light layer of soil.
Water, and place in a sunny spot. Mist daily, and soon you will be able to hide eggs, bunnies, and chicks among the soft blades.

mother's day *luncheon*

ARTICHOKE SOUP

1 medium onion, chopped
4 tablespoons butter
2 (13.5-ounce) cans
    artichoke hearts
1 cup milk, divided
2 cans cream of mushroom soup
2 cans cream of celery soup
1 can chicken broth
1 teaspoon worcestershire sauce
¼ cup parmesan cheese, grated
¼ teaspoon white pepper
(Do not add salt)

Sauté onion in butter in a Dutch oven until soft. Drain artichokes thoroughly, then rinse, quarter, and peel off outer leaves. Put artichokes in a food processor with ¼ cup milk, and purée. Add puréed artichokes and all other ingredients to onions. Heat to just below boiling point. Reduce heat, and simmer until ready to serve. Yield: 8-10 servings.

HERB CHEESE BISCUITS

1¾ cups all-purpose flour
½ teaspoon salt
2 teaspoons baking powder
⅓ cup vegetable shortening
½ tablespoon Italian herbs
½ cup cheddar cheese, grated
½ cup plain yogurt
½ cup milk
2 tablespoons butter, melted

Preheat oven to 450 degrees. Grease a baking sheet, and set aside. Combine flour, salt, and baking powder in a mixing bowl. Using a pastry blender, cut shortening into flour mixture until it resembles peas. Stir in herbs and grated cheese. Add yogurt and milk. Stir until it forms a soft dough. Turn dough onto a lightly floured surface; pat down to a ½-inch thickness. Cut out with a floured biscuit cutter, and place on the greased baking sheet. Brush tops with melted butter. Bake for about 12 minutes, then place under broiler for about 2 minutes to brown. Yield: about 16.

Use inexpensive clear glass candy dishes with tops for soup bowls. Tie flowers to the top with a ribbon bow.

CRAB CAKES WITH CAPER SAUCE

¼ cup green bell pepper, finely chopped
1 tablespoon oil
1 egg, lightly beaten
2 tablespoons mayonnaise
1 teaspoon Dijon mustard
⅛ teaspoon Old Bay seasoning
Salt to taste
⅛ teaspoon white pepper
1 pound lump crabmeat
⅓ cup fresh white breadcrumbs
¼ cup butter

Sauté bell pepper in oil until wilted, and set aside. In a mixing bowl, combine egg, mayonnaise, mustard, Old Bay seasoning, salt, and pepper. Add sautéed bell pepper, and mix well.

Pick crabmeat for shells. Place in a bowl, and sprinkle with breadcrumbs. Mix lightly. Pour egg mixture over crabmeat and breadcrumb mixture. Gently fold ingredients together, taking care not to break up lumps of crabmeat. Chill up to 1 hour before cooking.

Preheat oven to 350 degrees. Form cakes with ice cream scoop or your hands. Sauté cakes in butter in a skillet over medium heat, about 2 minutes on each side, until lightly browned. Place on a baking sheet, and bake for about 10 minutes or until cooked through. Serve with Caper Sauce. Yield: about 6.

CAPER SAUCE:

1 cup mayonnaise
1 tablespoon capers, drained
⅛ teaspoon worcestershire sauce
1 tablespoon fresh lemon juice
Cilantro, chopped (optional)

Combine all ingredients in a medium bowl, and whisk together. Refrigerate.

GRILLED VEGETABLES WITH TOASTED SESAME SEEDS

1 pound fresh asparagus, trimmed
1 tomato, cut into wedges
2 yellow squash, cut into rounds
4 ounces snow peas
½ cup olive oil
Salt and black pepper to taste
Sesame seeds, toasted

Toss vegetables with olive oil, salt, and pepper. Grill for 2-3 minutes, or lightly sauté in a skillet, or bake in a foil pack in the oven for about 10-15 minutes. Sprinkle with sesame seeds. Yield: 6 servings.

BERRIES IN A CLOUD

WHITE CHOCOLATE MERINGUE SHELLS:

3 large eggs whites, at room temperature
½ teaspoon vanilla
¼ teaspoon cream of tartar
1 cup sugar
1 ounce white chocolate baking squares, finely grated

Let egg whites stand at room temperature in a large mixing bowl for about 30 minutes. Preheat oven to 300 degrees. Cover a baking sheet with foil; draw eight 3-inch circles for individual shells or two 8-inch circles for large shells. Add vanilla and cream of tartar to egg whites. Beat with an electric mixer on medium speed until soft peaks form (tips curl). Add sugar, 1 tablespoon at a time, beating on high speed, until stiff peaks form (tips stand straight) and sugar is almost dissolved. Fold in grated white chocolate. Spread or pipe meringue over circles on foil, building up the edges to shape into shells. Bake for 30 minutes. Turn oven off; let dry in oven with door closed for at least 1 hour (do not open door). Peel off foil. Store in airtight container. Yield: 8 small or 2 large shells.

FILLING:

¾ (8-ounce) package reduced-fat
  cream cheese, softened
½ cup light dairy sour cream
2 tablespoons sugar
½ teaspoon Mexican vanilla
½ (8-ounce) container whipped topping
1 ounce semi-sweet chocolate, chopped
½ teaspoon vegetable shortening
3 to 4 cups small to medium strawberries, hulled
¼ cup strawberry jelly
1 to 2 teaspoons water

Beat together cream cheese, sour cream, sugar, and vanilla until smooth. Fold in whipped topping. Spread evenly in White Chocolate Meringue Shells. Cover, and chill for about 1 hour. Melt chocolate with shortening in a small, heavy saucepan; cool. Drizzle over sides of filled shells. Arrange berries, hulled ends down, over cream cheese filling. Heat jelly in a saucepan until melted, adding water to thin. Drizzle over arranged berries. Yield: 8 servings.

Set individual tables with
small flower arrangements
in teapots and teacups.

RIBBON ROSES FOR NAPKINS

You will find many uses for these simple ribbon roses. They are great on hand towels as well as napkins. They can be pinned to the corners of tablecloths or even all the way around the border. They also add a designer touch to towels, towel wraps, and slippers.

You will need:

10 inches green French wired ribbon
15 inches rose-colored French wired ribbon
Needle and thread
Safety pins

To form leaves, make a loop of green ribbon, and sew together in the center. For flower, gather rose-covered ribbon into a circle, connecting the base of the circle. Attach securely to the center of the leaf loop with several stitches, then pin into place with a safety pin on the underside for easy removal when washing.

Incorporate the color pink into your decorating scheme wherever possible.

Enjoy using silver teapots and sterling flatware everyday. They will achieve a beautiful patina and will rarely need polishing. Just make sure to wash by hand with a mild detergent and to dry thoroughly with a soft cloth.

CHOCOLATE TORTE

1 cup semi-sweet chocolate morsels
1 cup blanched whole almonds
2½ sticks butter
1½ cups sugar
3 eggs
1 scant cup all-purpose flour
½ cup water
2 tablespoons powdered cocoa
Dash salt
Confectioner's sugar
Whipped cream

Preheat oven to 350 degrees. Coat a 10-inch round springform pan with non-stick cooking spray. Line with parchment paper, then coat paper with butter. Combine chocolate morsels and almonds in a food processor, and process until ground, set aside. In a large mixing bowl, cream together butter and sugar until light and fluffy. Add eggs, 1 at a time, beating well after each addition. Add chocolate mixture, and beat well. Beat in flour.

Bring water almost to a simmer. Stir in cocoa and salt until dissolved. Remove from heat; allow to cool slightly. Add cocoa mixture to the bowl, and beat until well-blended. Pour batter into the prepared pan, and place on a cookie sheet. Bake for 55-60 minutes or until a toothpick inserted in the center comes out clean. Cool in the pan on a rack for 1 hour. Remove the pan sides, then sprinkle the torte with confectioner's sugar. Serve with whipped cream. Yield: 12 servings.

FRUIT TEA

4 quarts water, divided
2 cups sugar
2 large cinnamon sticks
2 family-size tea bags
½ cup lemon juice
2 cups pineapple juice
1 cup orange juice (not from concentrate)

Boil 2 quarts water, sugar, and cinnamon sticks for 2 minutes. Set aside. Boil 1 quart water; steep with tea bags for about 10 minutes. Cool, and discard tea bags. Mix 1 quart water, lemon juice, pineapple juice, and orange juice. Combine the three mixtures. Remove cinnamon sticks. Serve hot or cold. Yield: a gallon plus.

Use Grandmother's china or silver to show your love for tradition. Include all granddaughters in the party to reinforce the love of family.

MOTHER'S DAY TRAY FROM A VINTAGE FRAME

Make Mother or any loved one feel special by giving her a tray made from a lovely vintage frame. Set the tray with a small bud vase, vintage china, silver, and a monogrammed or embroidered napkin, and take her breakfast in bed.

Even after the special day, it may be used to serve afternoon tea or an assortment of desserts at a party. A mirrored tray could reflect a beautiful floral arrangement as a plateau for the center of the dining table or could be used as a dresser tray for perfume and jewelry.

You will need:
Vintage frame
Mirror or glass, cut to size
Small finishing nails
Fabric and backing
Quick Grab clear glue
Brown felt

Repair or paint the frame, if necessary. Have a mirror or glass cut to fit the frame. Secure the glass in place with small finishing nails. If you are using fabric, have a backing cut, and secure the fabric to the backing with a small amount of glue. Put in the glass first, then the fabric on backing. Secure the backing and glass with finishing nails. Glue felt to the back of the tray.

easy does it

graduation *tea*

QUICHE LORRAINE

CHICKEN SALAD IN
CREAM CHEESE SHELLS

WATERCRESS SANDWICHES
WITH BRIE AND WALNUTS

CHEESE STRAWS

POPPY SEED SCONES WITH
MOCK CLOTTED CREAM

BROWNIE BITES

CREAM CHEESE TARTS
WITH CHERRIES

SWEDISH ALMOND BARS

CHOCOLATE-DIPPED
STRAWBERRIES

BERRY SPRITZER

QUICHE LORRAINE

*8 ready-made small pie shells or
Pillsbury pie crust sheets for
mini tart shells
2 tablespoons real bacon bits
½ cup ham, shredded
8 slices Swiss cheese
3 eggs
½ cup half-and-half
½ teaspoon salt
¼ teaspoon black pepper
¼ teaspoon white pepper*

Preheat oven to 350 degrees. If making mini shells, cut out circle with biscuit cutter slightly larger than mini muffin tin. Press into lightly greased pan. Sprinkle bacon bits in bottoms of unbaked pie shells. Sprinkle each with ham and 1 slice of Swiss cheese broken into pieces. With an electric mixer, combine eggs, half-and-half, salt, and peppers, and mix well. Pour over cheese pieces into pie shell. Bake for about 20-25 minutes or until set. Yield: 8.

Make a menu card for each girl that tells the order of tea.
If all the courses of tea are on the table at once, scones or muffins are eaten first,
by breaking off one bite at a time, with jam and cream,
then small sandwiches, and finally, sweets.

CHICKEN SALAD IN CREAM CHEESE SHELLS

CREAM CHEESE SHELLS:

½ cup butter, softened
4 ounces cream cheese, softened
¼ teaspoon salt
¼ cup parmesan cheese, grated
1½ cups all-purpose flour

Preheat oven to 425 degrees. In a mixing bowl, beat together butter and cream cheese. Beat in salt and parmesan until well-combined. Beat in flour; knead dough into a ball. Shape into an 8-inch log. Cut into 24 slices. On a lightly floured surface, roll each slice into a 3-inch circle; press into a 2½-inch muffin cup. Bake for 5-7 minutes or until golden. Remove from pan when cool. Yield: 24.

CHICKEN SALAD:

2 large chicken breasts
1 quart buttermilk
½ cup sliced almonds
½ cup Hellman's mayonnaise
1 teaspoon lemon juice
Salt, black pepper, and white pepper to taste
Fresh parsley

Cook chicken breasts in buttermilk in a slow cooker on low for 2-3 hours. Chop chicken into small pieces, and set aside. Spread almonds on a cookie sheet, and toast in a 275-degree oven for about 7 minutes or until slightly brown. Combine chopped chicken, mayonnaise, lemon juice, salt, and peppers. Spoon into Cream Cheese Shells, and sprinkle with almonds and parsley.

Make chair-back covers by tying placemats to the backs of chairs with white satin bows.

For variety, use different colored flowers on the top of each tiered server.

WATERCRESS SANDWICHES WITH BRIE AND WALNUTS

12 thin slices wheat bread
4 tablespoons butter
6 ounces ripe Brie, rind removed and softened
2 tablespoons walnuts, toasted and chopped
Watercress, stems removed

Butter each slice of bread. Spread cheese on each slice. Sprinkle with walnuts, and place watercress on walnuts. Top with another slice of bread. Flatten slightly, and remove crusts. Cut into finger sandwiches. Yield: 18.

CHEESE STRAWS

2 cups extra-sharp cheddar cheese, grated
1 stick butter, softened
½ teaspoon salt
¼ teaspoon red pepper
1½ cups flour
Salt and paprika for sprinkling

Preheat oven to 325 degrees. Mix first 5 ingredients in a food processor to form a dough that is soft and pliable. Work with hands, and run through star disk of cookie press into long strips on a parchment-paper-lined baking sheet. Bake for 20-25 minutes. Cut into 3-inch pieces while still warm, but let cool on pan. Sprinkle lightly with salt and paprika. Store in an airtight container. Yield: about 6 dozen.

POPPY SEED SCONES

2 cups all-purpose flour
2½ teaspoons baking powder
¼ teaspoon salt
¼ cup sugar
4 tablespoons butter
¾ cup cream
1 tablespoon poppy seeds
2 teaspoons lemon zest
1 teaspoon lemon flavoring

Preheat oven to 400 degrees. Sift dry ingredients. Cut in butter until crumbly. Add cream, poppy seeds, zest, and lemon flavoring, and blend well; dough will be sticky. Flour a flat workspace, and knead dough for about half a minute. Roll out to ½ inch thick, and cut into desired shape (triangles are traditional). Bake for about 15 minutes. Yield: about 12.

MOCK CLOTTED CREAM

2 (8-ounce) packages cream cheese, softened
⅓ cup sugar
½ cup whipping cream
1 teaspoon vanilla

Whip all ingredients with a mixer until smooth and creamy. Refrigerate in a covered container.

BROWNIE BITES

1 (21.5-ounce) package brownie mix
1 (8-ounce) container sour cream
1 (12-ounce) package semi-sweet chocolate morsels
½ cup pecans, chopped
½ cup sugar
1 (16-ounce) can milk chocolate frosting

Preheat oven to 350 degrees. Prepare brownie mix according to package directions, but do not bake; add sour cream, chocolate morsels, and pecans. Pour into mini muffin tins that have been sprayed with non-stick cooking spray. Bake for about 10 minutes. Pour sugar onto plate. Dip bottoms and sides of brownies into sugar, and frost tops with canned chocolate frosting. Yield: about 36.

Set each table with different china, and use complementary cups and saucers.

CREAM CHEESE TARTS WITH CHERRIES

1 (8-ounce) package cream cheese, softened
1 (14-ounce) can sweetened condensed milk
⅓ cup lemon juice
1 teaspoon vanilla
24 small tart shells
1 can cherry pie filling

In a medium bowl, beat cream cheese until fluffy. Beat in sweetened condensed milk, lemon juice, and vanilla. Pour into crusts. Refrigerate for 4 hours, then top with cherry pie filling just before serving. Yield: 24.

SWEDISH ALMOND BARS

1 cup sliced almonds, divided
1 cup butter, melted
4 eggs
2 cups sugar
2 teaspoons almond extract
2½ cups all-purpose flour
½ teaspoon salt
3 tablespoons sugar
¼ teaspoon ground cinnamon

Preheat oven to 325 degrees. Sprinkle ½ cup almonds in the bottom of a greased and floured 10 x 15-inch jelly-roll pan. Beat butter and next 3 ingredients on medium speed until blended. Add flour and salt, beating until smooth; spread batter into prepared pan. Combine 3 tablespoons sugar and ground cinnamon; sprinkle evenly over cookie dough. Top with remaining ½ cup almonds. Bake for 30-35 minutes. Cool, and cut into bars. Yield: 36.

CHOCOLATE-DIPPED STRAWBERRIES

Fresh strawberries
8 ounces fine quality white chocolate, chopped
8 ounces fine quality milk, dark, semi-sweet,
  or bittersweet chocolate, chopped

Choose firm, delicious berries. Wipe with a soft pastry brush or cloth, and set aside on a paper towel to allow any moisture to be absorbed. Even a drop of moisture can cause chocolate to seize and harden.

Chocolate can be melted in a microwave oven or double boiler. For microwave, place broken chocolate pieces in a glass bowl. For bittersweet or semi-sweet chocolate, heat on medium for about 2 minutes per 4 ounces of chocolate. Milk chocolate or white chocolate should be melted on low for about 3 minutes per 4 ounces. Check chocolate halfway through cooking time, and check frequently to avoid scorching or burning. Chocolate will not change shape but will begin to look shiny and must be stirred until melted and smooth.

To melt chocolate in a double boiler, place top pan containing broken chocolate pieces over water when it begins boiling; turn off heat immediately. Allow to melt slowly, stirring frequently until smooth. To thin chocolate, add a small amount of vegetable shortening.

Hold berries by stems, and dip about two-thirds into chocolate. Allow to drip, and place on a cookie sheet lined with waxed paper to dry. Refrigerate fruit for about 20 minutes or until chocolate is set.

BERRY SPRITZER

1 (2-liter) bottle 7-Up
2 regular-size Wild Berry Zinger tea bags
Raspberries, strawberries, and mint for garnish

Pour about ¼ cup 7-Up from bottle. Add tea bags to bottle of remaining drink. Chill overnight. Serve over crushed ice with raspberries, strawberries, and mint. Yield: 8 servings.

easy does it

TEA CUP GIFTS

Start a lifelong collection of antique tea cups. You might want to tie a Bible verse to each cup for wisdom.

You will need:
Tea cups
Candy
Tulle
Ribbon
Small flowers

Fill each tea cup with candy, and wrap in tulle. Tie with a ribbon, and add flowers. Present one to each graduate.

Collect beautiful antique teapots and tea cups.
Share them as gifts with special friends.
Display your collection, but don't forget
to use them when friends drop by for tea.

TEA CUP BOOKMARKS

Let the girls make their own, or give them each a beaded bookmark with a special book as a gift.

You will need
Tea cups, teapots, and other charms
Beads
Ribbons

Tie several different lengths of ribbons together with a knot at the top. Intersperse beads, securing each with a knot along the ribbon. End each ribbon with a charm tied securely into place.

easy does it

Summer

Bright **sunshine** seems to linger on days of leisure.
It is a Southern tradition to share conversation,
chicken salad, and iced tea with long-time friends
among antique roses in a well-tended garden.
It is a simple pleasure to see **vine-ripened** vegetables
and fresh fruit displayed in baskets beside
homemade signs scrawled in childlike letters.
Glorious summer is here for a visit!

brunch by the pool

BRUNCH CASSEROLE

CHEESE GRITS

CRISPY BROCCOLI SALAD

FRESH FRUIT BOWL WITH
SPICED FRUIT DRESSING

MIMI'S KAHLUA BROWNIES
OR CHOCOLATE
NUT CLUSTERS

STRAWBERRY PECAN CAKE

BRUNCH CASSEROLE

½ stick margarine
8 to 10 slices white bread, crusts trimmed
1 pound hot pork sausage, cooked,
   crumbled, and drained
1 pound sharp cheddar cheese, shredded
6 eggs, beaten
1 cup milk
1 cup half-and-half
1 teaspoon dry mustard
¼ teaspoon black pepper
¼ teaspoon white pepper
Paprika for garnish

   Melt margarine in a 9 x 13-inch Pyrex dish, and line with bread. Sprinkle sausage over bread. Sprinkle cheese over sausage. Beat eggs, milk, half-and-half, mustard, and peppers. Pour over cheese, sausage, and bread. Cover, and refrigerate overnight. Preheat oven to 350 degrees, and bake for 45-50 minutes. Garnish with paprika. Yield: 10-12 servings.

Combine vegetables and fruits with blooming plants for a special centerpiece.
Ornamental **cabbage** comes in many nice colors; there is even a lime
and white variegated variety that resembles large, **ruffled** roses.
Tuck a few pretty pears into the base of the arrangement.

CHEESE GRITS

2 teaspoons salt
7 cups water
2 cups grits, uncooked
6 ounces Velveeta processed cheese
1 (6-ounce) roll Kraft garlic cheese
¼ cup jalapeños, drained and finely chopped
1 cup butter, melted
4 eggs, well-beaten
½ cup milk
1 tablespoon worcestershire sauce
Salt, black pepper, and white pepper to taste
Paprika for garnish

Add salt to boiling water, and cook grits, covered, over low heat until done, about 25 minutes. Cut cheeses into small pieces; stir into grits. Stir in jalapeños, butter, eggs, milk, worcestershire sauce, salt, and peppers. Spoon into a 3-quart casserole dish, and bake in a preheated 350-degree oven for 1 hour. Garnish with paprika. Yield: 12-16 servings.

CRISPY BROCCOLI SALAD

1 bunch fresh broccoli, cut into small pieces
2 hard-boiled eggs, grated
1 cup shredded Mexican mix cheese
2 green onions, chopped
1 to 2 tablespoons sunflower seeds
Approximately ½ cup ranch dressing
Real bacon bits

Mix together first 6 ingredients. Just before serving, top with bacon bits. Yield: 10-12 servings.

FRESH FRUIT BOWL WITH SPICED FRUIT DRESSING

Peel, slice, and toss together any combination of the following fruits:
Peaches, grapes, watermelon, blueberries, honeydew, cantaloupe, strawberries, pineapple, bananas, kiwis
Serve with Spiced Fruit Dressing.

SPICED FRUIT DRESSING:
½ cup white wine
½ cup honey
½ teaspoon cinnamon
¼ teaspoon allspice
3 tablespoons amaretto liqueur
3 tablespoons chopped fresh mint for garnish

Combine all ingredients except mint, and pour over fruit. Chill for several hours. Garnish with mint. Yield: 20 servings.

easy does it

GLASS CONTAINERS WITH FRUIT OR LEAVES

Add a delightful touch to a floral arrangement by using fruit or leaves in a glass container as the base. Fruit can be placed in the vase without water, and the arrangement can be made on top of the container on a base plate holding floral foam and flowers; alternately, the fruit in water can serve as the mechanics for the arrangement. Citrus fruit can even be sliced to reveal the beauty of the inside of the fruit. Or artfully swirl leaves inside a vase or submerge a small branch with leaves and berries in water. You can achieve lots of beautiful color combinations: limes are especially nice with pink or white flowers, and a simple arrangement of white tulips or lilies with cranberries offers understated elegance during the Christmas season.

MIMI'S KAHLUA BROWNIES

CRUST:
⅓ cup light brown sugar, firmly packed
5⅓ tablespoons unsalted butter, at room temperature
⅔ cup all-purpose flour, sifted
½ cup pecans, finely chopped

Preheat oven to 350 degrees. Grease and flour a 9-inch square baking pan. Cream sugar and butter until light and fluffy. Slowly add flour, and continue to mix until blended. Add pecans. When completely combined, press crust into the bottom of the prepared pan, and set aside.

FILLING:
2 ounces unsweetened chocolate
¼ cup vegetable shortening
4 tablespoons unsalted butter
2 large eggs
½ cup sugar
½ cup light brown sugar, firmly packed
1 teaspoon vanilla extract
¼ cup Kahlua liqueur
½ cup all-purpose flour, sifted
¼ teaspoon salt
½ cup pecans, chopped

Combine chocolate, shortening, and butter in a small saucepan over low heat. Stir until chocolate is melted and mixture is smooth. Cool. Combine eggs, sugars, and vanilla in a large bowl. Mix until blended. Stir into cooled chocolate mixture. Add Kahlua. Slowly add flour and salt, mixing until batter is smooth. Stir in pecans. Pour filling over prepared crust. Bake for 25 minutes or until tester inserted in center comes out clean. Be careful not to over-bake. While cooling, prepare Buttercream Frosting.

BUTTERCREAM FROSTING:
6 tablespoons unsalted butter, at room temperature
2 cups confectioner's sugar, sifted
1 tablespoon Kahlua liqueur
1 tablespoon heavy whipping cream

Cream all ingredients in a small bowl until smooth and creamy. Spread over cooled filling mixture, and refrigerate for 30 minutes. More Kahlua may be added to make spreading easier. For less sweet brownies, use only half of frosting.

GLAZE:
2 ounces semi-sweet chocolate
1 ounce unsweetened chocolate
2 teaspoons solid vegetable shortening

Melt chocolates and shortening over low heat, stirring constantly. Cool, and spread over Buttercream Frosting.

CHOCOLATE NUT CLUSTERS

1 (24-ounce) package almond bark
1 (12-ounce) package semi-sweet chocolate chips
1 (24-ounce) can salted peanuts

In a large microwave-safe bowl, heat almond bark and chips on defrost until melted, 2 minutes at a time for about 6 minutes. Stir in peanuts, and spoon onto waxed paper in small mounds. Yield: about 36.

Attach labels with the names of individual dishes to **lemons** or limes, using double-sided tape, and place next to each dish on the buffet table.

Strawberry Pecan Cake

STRAWBERRY PECAN CAKE

1 box white cake mix
1 (3-ounce) box strawberry Jell-O
1 cup vegetable oil
½ cup milk
4 eggs
1 cup frozen strawberries, slightly thawed
1 cup coconut
1 cup pecans, chopped

Preheat oven to 350 degrees. Mix cake mix and Jell-O together (dry). Add oil and milk, beating at moderate speed. Add eggs, 1 at a time. Then add strawberries, coconut, and pecans. Pour into a greased and floured 9 x 13-inch baking pan. (For two layers, make a second recipe.) Bake for 25 minutes. Let cool. Top with Icing

ICING:

1 stick margarine, softened
8 ounces cream cheese, softened
1 box confectioner's sugar
⅛ cup strawberries, drained
½ cup pecans
½ cup coconut

Cream margarine and cream cheese with confectioner's sugar. Add remaining ingredients. Beat until well-mixed. (To frost a two-layer cake, prepare a second recipe.)

For a small arrangement, place flowers in a can fitted with floral foam, then line the outside of the can with fresh asparagus spears. Secure spears in place with a rubber band concealed by raffia or a French wired ribbon tied in a bow.

ladies for

AVOCADO ON WHEAT
SANDWICHES

CHEDDAR-NUT
STRAWBERRY
SANDWICHES

CHICKEN SALAD
ON A PINEAPPLE RING
OR AVOCADO-DILL
CHICKEN SALAD

MARBLEIZED RASPBERRY
NUT SCONES

FRESH PEACH PIE OR
PEACHES AND CREAM CAKE

AVOCADO ON WHEAT SANDWICHES

1 ripe avocado
½ teaspoon lemon juice
Salt and white pepper to taste
3 tablespoons butter, softened
4 large slices whole wheat bread
2 tablespoons bacon bits

Peel avocado. Cut in half, and remove seed. In a bowl, mash avocado, then stir in lemon juice, salt, and pepper.

Butter bread. Spread avocado mixture on buttered sides of 2 bread slices. Scatter bacon bits over avocado. Cover with remaining bread slices, buttered sides down, and press together. Trim crusts, and cut each sandwich into 4 triangles. Yield: 8.

Always serve the guest of **honor** first.

As a general rule, serve prepared plates from the left and clear them from the right.

Pass food at the table to the right.

TULIPS IN CYLINDERS

Fill cylinders with water and 3 to 5 tulips standing straight and tall with only one head peeping out. Line cylinders down the center of a table for a dramatic appearance.

easy does it

FLOWER BALLS

Cover floral foam cylinders with daisies, mums, carnations, or roses. Place the flower balls on pedestals with green leaves at the base or directly on the table on a bed of green leaves and moss.

CHEDDAR-NUT STRAWBERRY SANDWICHES

8 ounces cheddar cheese, finely grated
2 tablespoons mayonnaise
2 tablespoons pecans, finely chopped
Salt, black pepper, and white pepper to taste
20 slices white bread
Strawberry preserves

Mix cheese, mayonnaise, pecans, salt, and peppers together well. Spread 10 slices of bread with cheese mixture and 10 slices with strawberry preserves. Put bread slices together with cheese mixture and strawberry preserves facing each other. Trim crusts, and cut into fingers. Yield: 30.

CHICKEN SALAD ON A PINEAPPLE RING

2 chicken breasts, cooked and diced
¼ teaspoon salt
Black pepper and white pepper to taste
Juice of ½ lemon
½ (8-ounce) can crushed pineapple, well-drained between paper towels
½ cup mayonnaise
2 tablespoons sliced almonds, lightly toasted
½ cup celery, diced
2 pineapple slices
Leaf lettuce

Combine chicken, salt, peppers, lemon juice, crushed pineapple, and mayonnaise; mix well. Blend in toasted almonds and celery. Place each pineapple slice on leaf lettuce, and top with chicken salad. Best if made as close to serving time as possible. Yield: 2 servings.

AVOCADO-DILL CHICKEN SALAD

4 boneless, skinless chicken breasts
1 can chicken broth
1 (3-ounce) package cream cheese
4 tablespoons mayonnaise
2 tablespoons lemon juice
½ teaspoon lemon zest
¼ teaspoon salt
¼ teaspoon white pepper
2 tablespoons fresh dill, snipped

Place chicken breasts and broth in a saucepan, and add water to cover. Simmer, covered, for 30 minutes or until tender. Refrigerate in broth until cool. Meanwhile, make dressing by beating together cream cheese, mayonnaise, and lemon juice. Add lemon peel, salt, pepper, and dill. Remove chicken from refrigerator, drain broth, and cut chicken into bite-sized pieces. Stir chicken chunks into dressing.

To Assemble:
Romaine lettuce
6 Roma tomatoes, sliced
1 avocado, sliced into strips
Seasoned salt
Fresh dill, snipped
Italian dressing
Sliced almonds, toasted

Place a bed of romaine on each plate; top with alternating Roma tomato slices and avocado slices in a circle. Sprinkle with seasoned salt and dill. Drizzle with Italian dressing. Place a large scoop of chicken salad in the center, and sprinkle with toasted almonds. Yield: about 6 servings.

MARBLEIZED RASPBERRY NUT SCONES

2 cups flour, plus more for rolling
2½ teaspoons baking powder
¼ teaspoon salt
¼ cup sugar
4 tablespoons butter
¾ cup whipping cream
1 cup fresh or frozen raspberries, rolled in flour
½ cup pecans, chopped

Preheat oven to 400 degrees. Sift dry ingredients together. Using a food processor, cut in butter until crumbly. Add cream, and blend well; dough will be sticky. Blend in flour-coated raspberries and pecans. Flour a flat work surface, and knead dough for about a minute. Roll out to about ½ inch thick, and cut into shapes. Bake for 15 minutes. Serve with jam and cream. Yield: about 12-16 scones.

A choice of **salads** will allow friends to create their own sampler plates.
    Serve with a variety of small sandwiches or crackers.

Let guests change tables for **dessert**
so they can visit with a new group of friends.

FRESH PEACH PIE

2 (7-inch) pie shells
¾ cup sugar
2½ tablespoons cornstarch
¾ cup water
1 (3-ounce) package sugar-free peach-flavored gelatin
¼ teaspoon almond extract
4 cups fresh Indian red peaches, peeled
1 tablespoon lemon juice
1 (8-ounce) container whipped topping

Bake pie shells according to package directions, and set aside. Combine sugar, cornstarch, and water in a saucepan, and cook over medium heat until thickened. Add gelatin and almond extract, and cool. Slice peaches, and sprinkle with lemon juice. Fold peaches into cooled gelatin mixture. Divide, and pour into pie shells. Cover with whipped topping, and chill. Yield: 2 pies.

PEACHES AND CREAM CAKE

1 box butter-recipe yellow cake mix
1½ cups sugar
4 tablespoons cornstarch
4 cups fresh peaches, chopped
½ cup water
1 cup sour cream
2 cups whipping cream
2 to 3 tablespoons confectioner's sugar
Fresh sliced peaches for garnish

Prepare cake mix in two layers according to package directions. Cool and split each layer. Combine sugar and cornstarch in a saucepan. Add peaches and water. Cook over medium heat, stirring constantly, until smooth and thickened. Cool. Spoon ¼ of peach filling over each layer of cake. Spread ¼ cup sour cream over filling. Repeat. Combine whipping cream and confectioner's sugar in mixing bowl, and beat until stiff peaks form. Frost cake with sweetened cream, and garnish with sliced peaches. Yield: 16-20 servings.

Consider ease of **conversation** during the meal. A good rule for centerpieces at seated dinners is to keep them tall and thin enough to see between or low enough to see over.

SIMPLE CENTERPIECES

Quick and easy centerpieces can be created with a minimal number of flowers. Line the dining table with an odd number of goblets that are centered on dessert plates. Place a hand-gathered nosegay in each goblet, and arrange short-stemmed blossoms, buds, and leaves at the base on each plate. Intertwine ivy, tree fern, smilax, or other greenery among the arrangements. Round bowls filled with mixed flowers and placed on glass candleholders of various heights also make great containers for table groupings.

easy does it

rose garden *luncheon*

CHICKEN CHOW MEIN

HOT PEACH CASSEROLE

GREEN SALAD WITH
FRUIT AND FLOWERS

EASY ROLLS

RICH CHOCOLATE
MOUSSE WITH
CHOCOLATE-DIPPED
ROSE PETALS AND
BUTTER CRISP COOKIES
OR EASY TIRAMISU

CHICKEN CHOW MEIN

3 tablespoons onion, chopped
1 cup celery, chopped
2 tablespoons butter
4 cups cooked chicken, chopped
1 can cream of mushroom soup
1 can cheddar cheese soup
1 (5-ounce) can evaporated milk
1 (16-ounce) can French-style green beans
1 (2-ounce) jar chopped pimientos
½ cup toasted almonds, sliced
1 (8-ounce) can sliced water chestnuts
1 (3-ounce) can chow mein noodles
1 teaspoon salt
Toasted sliced almonds for garnish

Preheat oven to 350 degrees. Sauté onions and celery in butter until translucent. Add next 10 ingredients, and mix well. Spoon into a greased casserole dish. Sprinkle almonds on top. Bake at 350 degrees for 45 minutes. Yield: 12 servings.

To dine in a **rose garden** is a magnificent and unforgettable experience filled with fragrance and beauty.

HOT PEACH CASSEROLE

2 (16-ounce) cans peach halves
¼ cup butter
½ box light brown sugar
3 tablespoons lemon juice
1 small box Cheese Nips crackers, crushed

Drain peaches, and place cavity side up in a greased casserole dish. Melt butter, and add sugar. Add lemon juice, and pour mixture over peach halves. Refrigerate overnight. Preheat oven to 350 degrees. Just before baking, sprinkle with crushed crackers. Bake, uncovered, for 40-45 minutes. Yield: 8-10 servings.

GREEN SALAD WITH FRUIT AND FLOWERS

½ cup walnuts, coarsely chopped
2 tablespoons butter
1 head Bibb lettuce, washed and torn into
* bite-sized pieces*
½ pound fresh spinach, washed and torn into
* bite-sized pieces*
2 green onions, sliced
1 pint fresh strawberries, washed and sliced
18 pesticide-free Johnny-jump-ups or pansies

Sauté walnuts in butter until lightly browned. Toss lettuce, spinach, green onions, and browned walnuts. Sprinkle with strawberries and flowers. Drizzle with Sweet and Sour Dressing.

SWEET AND SOUR DRESSING:
1 cup vegetable oil
¾ cup sugar
½ cup white wine vinegar
2 tablespoons soy sauce
¼ teaspoon salt
¼ teaspoon black pepper
¼ teaspoon white pepper

Combine all ingredients, and drizzle over salad.

EASY ROLLS

1 package yeast
⅓ cup warm water
2 tablespoons sugar
2 cups milk, warmed
¾ cup oil
5 cups self-rising flour
2 tablespoons butter, melted

Mix yeast and warm water; add sugar. Add warm milk and oil. Sift 4 cups of flour into mixture, and blend with a slotted spoon. Add remaining cup of flour until mixture is stiff. Place half of dough on a floured surface, and knead 4 or 5 times. Flatten a tablespoon of dough at a time with hand, and place in a greased muffin tin. Repeat with remaining dough. Let rise for 30 minutes. Brush tops with melted butter. Bake in a preheated 400-degree oven for 15 minutes. Dough may be refrigerated in a tightly covered container for 2 weeks. Yield: about 2 dozen.

RICH CHOCOLATE MOUSSE WITH CHOCOLATE-DIPPED ROSE PETALS AND BUTTER CRISP COOKIES

3 large eggs, separated
7 ounces semi-sweet chocolate
1 (4-ounce) bar German sweet chocolate
2 teaspoons amaretto liqueur
¼ cup sugar
Whipped topping
Pesticide-free rose petals dipped in almond bark
   for garnish

Beat egg yolks until thick and lemony. Set aside egg whites. While beating the yolks, melt chocolate in the top of a double boiler or in microwave, then add amaretto. Cool slightly, then slowly add chocolate to beaten yolks. Set this aside. Whip egg whites and sugar until peaks form; fold into chocolate mixture, and pour into individual dishes. Chill for at least 5 hours or overnight. Return to room temperature before serving. Top with whipped topping and chocolate-dipped rose petals. Serve with Butter Crisp Cookies. Yield: 6 servings.

To make chocolate-dipped rose petals, cut off the small white piece that attached the petal to the rose. Melt a small amount of almond bark in the microwave, and dip the edge of each petal into the chocolate. Allow the petals to dry on waxed paper.

BUTTER CRISP COOKIES:

1 cup butter
1 cup sugar
1 teaspoon vanilla
1 tablespoon water
1 egg
2½ cups flour
2 teaspoons baking powder
1 cup pecans, chopped

Cream butter and sugar. Add vanilla, water, and egg; beat well. Combine flour and baking powder, and add to creamed mixture. Beat well. Stir in pecans. Roll dough into 2-inch rolls. Chill in waxed paper in refrigerator for at least 1 hour. Cut into ¼-inch slices, and place cookies on a parchment-lined baking sheet. Bake in a preheated 350-degree oven for 10-15 minutes. Yield: about 48.

Make rose and citrus **potpourri** by combining 9 ounces of dried scented rose petals, 3½ ounces of dried lavender, and the grated peel of 2 lemons. Leave in an airtight container for 2 to 3 days, then add 1 teaspoon each of ground allspice and orris root, and shake well. Leave potpourri for a week, stirring occasionally. Place a few scoops in netting to give as favors.

ROSE-GATHERING CONTAINER

Make this simple flower-gathering helper for your favorite gardener.

You will need:
⅜-inch wooden dowel, cut to about
   23 inches long
3 large juice cans
Spray metal primer
Metallic paint
3 wood screws
Liquid Nails glue
Plastic-coated bicycle hook

Cut the dowel to the desired length. Paint the dowel and the three cans (inside and outside) with primer and then with metallic paint. Drill a small hole in each can near the top, varying the distances from the top ½ to 2 inches. Screw each can to the dowel, making sure they will be level on the bottom. Glue the cans to the length of the dowel with the Liquid Nails for stability. Drill a hole into the top of the dowel, and screw in the bicycle hook for a handle. Fill the cans with several inches of water, and head to the rose garden.

Scatter rose **petals** on the table
to add a feminine touch.
They can also be spread along the path leading to the table.

OPEN BOX OF ROSES

For a centerpiece container, fill an interesting box with roses.

You will need:
Box with a hinged lid
Waterproof green florist foil
Floral foam
Roses
Berries
Line an interesting hinged box with florist foil, and place a piece of wet floral foam inside. Layer roses and berries in foam, and gently close lid to reveal roses peeking from the box.

ROSE POTS

Line simple rose pots down a table for informal luncheons or formal dinners.

You will need:
Clay pots or antique English ash pots
Clear acrylic sealer
Duct tape
Waterproof green florist foil
Floral foam
6 to 7 roses per pot, depending on size
English boxwood sprigs
Seal each pot inside and out with clear acrylic sealer. Tape the hole on the bottom of the pot with duct tape. Shape foil to line the inside of the pot. Fit wet floral foam inside the foil. Place 5-6 roses around the outside edge of the pot, evenly spaced. Put a slightly longer-stemmed rose in the center of the pot. Fill in with boxwood sprigs.

Use fun, **contemporary** vases or goblets
with selected garden roses for the table, or place
miniature roses in clay pots tied with ribbons
to give as favors to the honored guests.
Make rose pots or rose topiaries,
or fill an **antique box** with roses and berries
peeping from the opened lid.

EASY TIRAMISU

⅓ cup cooled instant espresso or strong coffee, divided
2 packages ladyfingers
1 (8-ounce) package cream cheese
1 can sweetened condensed milk, divided
1 (12-ounce) container whipped topping
1 (12-ounce) package miniature chocolate
    chips, divided
Whipped topping, chocolate shavings, chocolate-
    dipped rose petals, mint leaves, berries, or sugared
    miniature rosebuds for garnish

Make and cool espresso. Brush all except one or two
tablespoons on split ladyfingers. Mix cream cheese,
remaining espresso, and ⅔ of condensed milk in mixer.
Fold in whipped topping and about half of the chocolate
chips. Heat remaining condensed milk in microwave.
Add remaining chocolate chips, and mix to make a
chocolate sauce. Layer ladyfingers in individual goblets
or in a trifle bowl. Add a layer of the espresso-chocolate
chip mixture, followed by some chocolate sauce.
Swirl with a knife. Repeat layers. (You may also add a
layer of whipped topping.) Chill thoroughly, and garnish
with whipped topping, chocolate shavings, chocolate-
dipped rose petals, mint, berries, or sugared miniature
rosebuds. Yield: 10 servings.

Garnish desserts with **sugared** pesticide-free roses
made by sprinkling sugar on rosebuds
that have been painted with beaten egg whites.

alfresco *dinner*

STEAK FAJITAS

BELL PEPPERS STUFFED
WITH CORN SALAD

SPICY TOMATO ASPIC

BLUEBERRY COBBLER
WITH HOMEMADE
VANILLA ICE CREAM

STEAK FAJITAS

1½ pounds boneless sirloin steak
Mr. Yoshida's Teriyaki EZ Marinader
   in a bag
2 tablespoons cooking oil, divided
2 large onions, julienned
2 large green bell peppers, julienned
6 (6-inch) flour tortillas
1 cup shredded Mexican mix cheese
Sour cream, shredded lettuce, and
   diced tomatoes for topping

Place steak in marinating bag, and refrigerate overnight. Remove steak from bag, and cut into ½-inch strips across the grain. Heat 1 tablespoon oil in a large skillet over medium heat. Add onions and bell pepper; sauté for 10 minutes or until tender. Remove from skillet, and heat 1 tablespoon oil on medium high heat; add steak. Brown 2 minutes on each side. Return vegetables to skillet with steak, and heat. Heat tortillas according to package directions. Fill warm tortillas with steak, vegetables, and cheese. Top with sour cream, lettuce, and diced tomatoes. Yield: 6.

BELL PEPPERS STUFFED WITH CORN SALAD

6 bell peppers, whole
4 cans whole white corn, drained
1 green bell pepper, diced
1 red bell pepper, diced
1 green onion, chopped
2 tomatoes, diced and drained
1 tablespoon mayonnaise or more to taste
Salt and black pepper to taste
Fresh leaf lettuce and spinach
Sliced mushrooms
1 red bell pepper, chopped
Pine nuts, toasted
Balsamic vinaigrette dressing

Cut tops off 6 bell peppers, and clean out membranes and seeds. Mix next 7 ingredients, and stuff peppers. Serve on a bed of leaf lettuce, spinach, mushrooms, chopped peppers, and pine nuts drizzled with balsamic vinaigrette. Yield: 6 servings.

SPICY TOMATO ASPIC

1 (14.5-ounce) can Mexican stewed tomatoes
1 (3-ounce) package red raspberry Jell-O
Fresh leaf lettuce

Purée tomatoes in food processor. Heat in microwave, then add Jell-O. Pour into greased molds, and refrigerate until congealed. Serve on a bed of leaf lettuce. Yield: 4.

Aged, **handmade** ladder-back chairs keep the rustic theme pure and simple for this pleasant outdoor entertaining setting.

BLUEBERRY COBBLER

2 cups water
2 cups sugar
1 stick butter
1½ cups self-rising flour
½ cup vegetable shortening
⅓ cup milk
3 cups fresh blueberries

Preheat oven to 350 degrees. Combine water and sugar in a saucepan, and boil for 4 minutes; set aside. Melt butter in an 8 x 11-inch baking dish; set aside. Combine flour, shortening, and milk to make pastry. Roll into a rectangle shape on a floured surface. Place blueberries on pastry; roll up in a jelly-roll fashion. Cut into 16 slices. Place side by side in the buttered dish, and pour syrup over the top. Bake for 45 minutes. Yield: 16 servings.

HOMEMADE VANILLA ICE CREAM

6 large eggs, beaten until foamy
2½ cups sugar
2 large cans evaporated milk
2 ounces vanilla extract
Enough whole milk to make a gallon

In a large Dutch oven, beat eggs, sugar, evaporated milk, and vanilla with a wire whisk. Add 2 quarts of whole milk, and simmer over medium heat until hot, stirring continuously from the bottom to keep from scorching, but do not boil. Let mixture cool, and pour into a 1-gallon ice cream freezer. Add more whole milk to fill the freezer container 1 inch from the top. Freeze ice cream according to freezer directions, layering the bucket with ice and ice cream salt alternately. For fruit ice cream, add about 1½ cups of fresh crushed fruit. Yield: 1 gallon.

DOOR TABLETOP

Use an old door for a tabletop. These legs are made from 4 sturdy strappy urns filled with wild materials such as dock and Queen Ann's Lace mixed with yard greenery in floral foam. Legs can also be made from sawhorses or concrete columns.

Architectural accents add a new dimension to decorating. Combining a rustic element with any setting creates a relaxed atmosphere.

Simple **striped** napkins are laid over the backs of the ladder-back chairs to emphasize the linear design.

SHUTTER FIRE SCREEN

Make a summer fire screen from aged shutters.

You will need:
3 small old shutters of the same height, or 1 small shutter
   and 1 tall shutter cut in half
Paint for base coat (I used "Buttermilk" by American)
4 small hinges
Paint for aging (I used "Wedgwood Green" and "Hippo Gray"
   by Delta Ceramcoat and "Sandstone" by Plaid)
Ornamental detail piece (available at craft stores)
Sandpaper, saw, drill, and screws

Cut shutters to the desired height, if necessary. Center shutter may be slightly taller. I used one center shutter and cut a tall shutter in half for the two sides; the height of each piece is about 30 inches.

Paint all shutters with a base coat. Sand with coarse sandpaper to reveal some of the original color and wood. Create a weathered appearance by lightly applying accents of other colors with a dry brush. Hinge the shutters together to make a trifold screen; paint hinges. Paint ornamental detail in the same manner as the shutters, then attach to the top of the center shutter with screws.

easy does it

MEDALLION COASTERS

Use architectural medallions to create interesting coasters.

You will need:
4 corner medallions (available at home improvement stores)
Paint (I used "Burnt Umber" and "Dolphin Gray" by Delta, "Antique Gold"
by Apple Barrel,
"Gooseberry Pink" by
American, and "Poetry
Green" by Plaid)
Gold marking pen
Sandpaper
Clear acrylic sealer
Felt
Elmer's wood glue

Paint medallions with burnt umber paint, allow to dry. Accent with the gold marking pen. Then paint each coaster a different color; allow to dry. Sand until the gold, umber, and wood show through for an aged appearance. Spray with clear acrylic sealer. Cut felt to fit the back of each coaster, and glue into place with wood glue.

The table is set with a combination of antique and reproduction **majolica pieces**. All the plates are different but are drawn together as a whole with the use of simple muted pottery chargers. Vividly colored summer yard flowers such as clematis and purple iris, along with vines and fruit, combine with antique majolica ducks and bubble glass goblets to complete the look.

PEDIMENT SHELF WITH SPOON AND FORK HOOKS

Display favorite collectibles on this architectural pediment shelf.

You will need:
Ornamental pediment from above a door
or window
Paint of your choice (I used "Sandstone"
by Plaid)
Paintbrushes
3 different silver-plated soup spoons
2 different silver-plated dinner or luncheon forks
Saw, sandpaper, rubber mallet, vise, drill,
and screws

Cut the pediment to the desired length (this one is about 32 inches long). Sand with very coarse sandpaper to reveal the old finish and wood. Apply a small amount of paint with a dry brush to enhance the finish. Sand again lightly. Using a rubber mallet, bend spoons and forks while holding them in a vise, creating hooks. Drill 2 tiny holes in the handle of each piece. Evenly space spoons and forks on the bottom of the pediment, and screw into place. Place cups and saucers or other decorative items on the shelf, and hang linen towels or napkins from the spoon and fork hooks.

candlelight *dinner*

SPINACH SALAD WITH DIJON VINAIGRETTE

6 slices bacon
1½ teaspoons Dijon mustard
1 tablespoon sugar
½ cup red wine vinegar
½ cup olive oil
1 bunch scallions, thinly sliced
Salt, freshly ground black pepper, and
    white pepper to taste
2 bunches fresh spinach, washed,
    drained, and torn into pieces
Fresh mushrooms, sliced
2 hard-boiled eggs, chopped
½ cup parmesan cheese, grated

Cook bacon slices until crisp. Drain, and crumble. Over medium heat, add Dijon mustard to the bacon drippings, and whisk until blended. Add sugar, and whisk until dissolved. Add red wine vinegar, and whisk to blend. Add olive oil, and blend. Toss in scallions, and sauté for 2 minutes only. Add salt and peppers to taste.

Toss spinach, mushrooms, crumbled bacon, eggs, and cheese in a wooden salad bowl. Add dressing, and toss. Serve at once. Yield: 8 servings.

Arrange serving plates to take advantage of **beautifully** colored vegetables and fruits. Different herbs and spices enhance the flavors of meats and vegetables while adding color, shape, and texture.

PARMESAN PITA TRIANGLES

3 pita bread rounds
6 tablespoons unsalted butter, melted
¾ cup parmesan cheese, freshly grated
Fresh parsley, chopped

   Preheat oven to broil. Cut around edge of each pita round, making 2 round halves. (There should be 6 rounds.) Cut each round into eight wedges. Place bread smooth side down on a baking sheet. Brush each section with melted butter. Sprinkle parmesan on top of each wedge. Sprinkle with parsley. Broil in oven until hot, golden brown, and bubbly. Yield: 48.

Plates and silver flatware should be placed about one inch from the table edge. Dessert forks may be placed above the plates with tines facing right. Butter knives are placed on top of bread and butter plates.

STUFFED CHICKEN BREASTS WITH ROASTED RED PEPPER SAUCE OVER RICE AND VEGETABLES

1 (8-ounce) package cream cheese, softened
⅓ cup parmesan cheese, grated
2 tablespoons capers, drained
2 tablespoons half-and-half
Dash white and black pepper
6 boneless, skinless chicken breasts
1 tablespoon olive oil
¼ cup dry white wine
6 servings Uncle Ben's Original long-grain rice, prepared
Chives and lemon zest for garnish

In a small mixing bowl, combine cream cheese, parmesan cheese, capers, half-and-half, and peppers; set aside. Rinse chicken breasts, and pat dry. Place each breast half between 2 pieces of plastic wrap. Working from the center to the edges, pound the chicken lightly with the flat side of a meat mallet to a ⅛-inch thickness. Remove plastic wrap. Spread a thin layer of cream cheese mixture over each breast half. Fold in the sides, and roll up jelly-roll style, pressing the edges to seal. In a large frying pan, heat olive oil. Brown chicken on both sides (about 5 minutes total). Transfer chicken to a 2-quart baking dish. Pour wine over the chicken. Bake, uncovered, in a preheated 350-degree oven for 20-25 minutes or until chicken is tender and no pink remains. Let cool, and cut into about 1-inch pinwheel rounds.

To serve, spoon rice into a mound in the center of the plate, and place chicken rounds on rice. Drizzle Roasted Red Pepper Sauce over chicken. Place Asparagus and Bell Peppers on top of chicken and rice mound. Garnish with chives and lemon zest.

ROASTED RED PEPPER SAUCE:

¾ cup (15.5-ounce bottle) roasted bell peppers, drained
1 tablespoon olive oil
½ cup half-and-half
1 tablespoon flour
1 tablespoon capers, drained

In a food processor, blend roasted bell peppers until smooth; set aside. In a small saucepan, heat olive oil. Add puréed peppers, half-and-half, flour, and drained capers. Heat through.

ASPARAGUS AND BELL PEPPERS:

1 pound (about 20 stalks) asparagus, trimmed
½ teaspoon salt
2 red bell peppers, seeded and sliced
2 yellow bell peppers, seeded and sliced

Drop trimmed asparagus into salted boiling water, and cook for 3-5 minutes. Remove immediately to a cool water bath.

Drop bell peppers into boiling water, and cook for about 3-5 minutes until crisp-tender.

Garnish desserts with berries, mint, and lemon curls.

MAYONNAISE BISCUITS

1½ cups Bisquick
2 rounded tablespoons mayonnaise
½ teaspoon sugar
½ cup half-and-half

Preheat oven to 450 degrees. Mix together all ingredients. Roll out with floured hands, and cut out with a 2-inch cookie cutter. Bake for about 12-15 minutes. Yield: 16.

LEMON TARTS IN COCONUT SHELLS

SHELLS:

2 cups sweetened shredded coconut
½ cup sugar
2 egg whites

Preheat oven to 325 degrees. Process coconut and sugar in a food processor until coconut is minced. Blend in egg whites. Press mixture into well-greased 4-inch tartlet pans with removable bottoms. Bake for 25-30 minutes or until golden. Remove from pans. Fill each crust with ¼ cup of Filling. Yield: 8.

FILLING:

2 teaspoons lemon zest, grated
1 cup sugar
5 egg yolks, beaten
½ cup fresh lemon juice
Dash salt
½ cup margarine, melted

Combine zest and sugar in a food processor. Pulse to mince zest, then process until very fine. Add beaten egg yolks, lemon juice, and salt. Process a few seconds. With the processor running, add margarine. Transfer to a double boiler, and cook over low heat, stirring continuously, until mixture reaches the consistency of mayonnaise. Store in a covered jar in refrigerator until ready to use. Will keep for weeks. Fills about 40 mini tartlets.

Combine flowers and fruits
for your table arrangement.
If you are using a large, extravagant arrangement
or a tall antique epergne,
make sure it is placed where guests
can see each other around it.

FRUITS AND VEGETABLES IN FLORAL ARRANGEMENTS

Add fruits and vegetables to your flowers. The shapes and beautiful colors will add a new depth to your table. They are beautiful whether left whole or cut to reveal the interiors.

BRUSSELS SPROUT ROSES

Make beautiful lime-colored "roses" from Brussels sprouts by gently pulling the leaves open one by one. Place "roses" in ice water until ready to use. Place them on wooden skewers, and insert into the arrangement.

FLOWER PETAL SKEWER

Make a skewer of fresh or pressed and dried rose petals and beads. Just thread them on a gold or silver wire, and insert into an arrangement.

easy does it

Autumn

Leaves color the pathway to my door.

It is delightful to discover foliage and berries to combine

with pumpkins, vegetables, and fruits for the table.

It is reflective to drink tea by the fireside and

share thoughts with someone whose face shines

and voice sings in the warm glow.

Pleasure is seeing my family

around the Thanksgiving table, giving thanks together

with faithful love and traditions.

sunflowers and *lunch*

CREAMY CHICKEN
ENCHILADAS

CONFETTI RICE

TOSSED GREENS WITH
RED BELL PEPPERS

MEXICAN
CINNAMON-COFFEE FLAN

CREAMY CHICKEN ENCHILADAS

1 tablespoon margarine
1 medium onion, chopped
1 (4.5-ounce) can chopped green
  chilies, drained
1 (8-ounce) package cream cheese, softened
  and cut into small pieces
1 can cream of chicken soup
3½ cups cooked chicken breasts, chopped
12 (8-inch) flour tortillas
1 (8-ounce) package Monterey Jack
  cheese, shredded
2 cups whipping cream

Preheat oven to 350 degrees. Melt margarine in a large skillet over medium heat; add onion, and sauté for 5 minutes. Add green chilies, and sauté for 1 minute. Stir in cream cheese, cream of chicken soup, and chicken. Cook, stirring constantly, until cream cheese melts. Spoon 2-3 tablespoons of chicken mixture down the center of each tortilla, and roll up. Place seam side down in a lightly greased 9 x 13-inch baking dish. Sprinkle with Monterey Jack cheese, and drizzle with whipping cream. Bake for 30-45 minutes. Yield: 12 enchiladas.

Use chopped bell peppers, parsley, and chives as confetti to add color to any Mexican dish.

CONFETTI RICE

½ medium onion, chopped
½ red bell pepper, chopped
½ yellow bell pepper, chopped
½ green bell pepper, chopped
1 small can chopped mushrooms, drained
1 stick margarine
1 cup rice
1 can chicken broth
1 cup water
½ cup slivered almonds, toasted

Sauté onion, bell peppers, and mushrooms in margarine. Combine vegetables, rice, broth, water, and almonds in a greased casserole dish. Bake in a preheated 350-degree oven for 45 minutes or until broth is absorbed. Yield: 8 servings.

TOSSED GREENS WITH RED BELL PEPPERS

Fresh baby spinach leaves
1 red bell pepper, chopped
½ cup cherry tomatoes, sliced
¼ cup real bacon bits
2 ounces goat cheese, crumbled

Toss vegetables. Drizzle with Balsamic Vinaigrette. Sprinkle with bacon bits and goat cheese. Yield: 6-8 servings.

BALSAMIC VINAIGRETTE:
⅓ cup balsamic vinegar
1 tablespoon Dijon mustard
1 tablespoon honey
¼ teaspoon poppy seeds
⅔ cup olive oil

Combine first 4 ingredients in a small saucepan. Whisk in oil, and bring to a boil over medium heat. Remove from heat. Serve slightly warm or at room temperature. Yield: 1 cup.

For a different look, position placemats vertically, or use unfolded square napkins as placemats.

MEXICAN CINNAMON-COFFEE FLAN

CINNAMON CARAMEL:

1 cup sugar
½ cup water
½ teaspoon ground cinnamon

Combine all ingredients in a small saucepan, and bring to a boil over medium heat, stirring constantly until sugar dissolves. Continue boiling, without stirring, until the syrup turns a medium golden brown, about 7-9 minutes. Immediately remove from heat, and divide equally among 6 custard cups, turning each cup to evenly coat bottom and sides.

COFFEE CUSTARD:

1 cup whipping cream
1 cup milk
2 heaping teaspoons instant coffee granules
1 teaspoon vanilla
3 eggs
2 egg yolks
½ cup brown sugar
Pinch salt

Heat whipping cream and milk in a medium saucepan over medium heat. As soon as the liquid is hot and begins to form bubbles at the side of the pan, remove from heat, and stir in coffee and vanilla. Meanwhile, in a mixing bowl, lightly beat eggs, egg yolks, brown sugar, and salt with a wire whisk until combined. Preheat oven to 325 degrees. Bring a kettle of water to a boil. Stirring continuously with the whisk, slowly pour 6 ounces of milk mixture into egg mixture. Pour this back into remaining milk, and stir to blend. Pour mixture into coated custard cups, and set in a baking dish. Pour boiling water into baking pan to come halfway up custard cups. Bake for about 20-25 minutes or until a small sharp knife inserted into the center of a flan comes out clean. Let cool at room temperature, then refrigerate. Before serving, run a small knife around the edge of each cup to loosen flan. Turn onto individual plates. Yield: 6.

Autumn is a great time to use sunflowers, olive jars, ornamental peppers, and berries.

SUNFLOWERS AND LADYBUGS

Display sunflower pots in groups of various sizes for a festive table or side-board presentation.

You will need:
Small clay pots
Clear acrylic sealer
Duct tape
Waterproof green
  florist foil
Floral foam
Large ivy leaves or galax leaves
1 sunflower per pot
Green organza ribbon
1 package wooden ladybugs
Glue

Prepare pots with sealer. Cover holes with duct tape, and line pots with foil. Place wet floral foam in each pot.

For tall sunflower, cover top of floral foam with leaves. Insert a sunflower with a 6- to 8-inch stem; tie a green organza ribbon into a bow with streamers just below the flower. Glue a playful ladybug to a green base leaf.

For flat sunflowers, cover the base with leaves, and insert a sunflower with a very short stem into the floral foam covered with leaves. Add a ladybug to the center of the sunflower.

easy does it

HERB OIL

Use herb oils for dipping breads and for salad dressings. To make herb oil, use a mild oil such as olive, peanut, safflower, or sunflower oil. Choose fresh herbs such as basil, thyme, tarragon, sage, oregano, or rosemary. Slightly bruise enough herb sprigs to fill the bottle about half full. Cover herbs with oil, and seal. Leave for about 2 weeks in a warm place, shaking once a day. Strain oil through cheesecloth, pressing the herbs, and taste. If you prefer a stronger flavor, repeat the process. When the oil achieves a flavor you like, strain oil, pour into bottles, and seal. Store oils for 2-4 weeks in the refrigerator.

HERB VINEGAR

Herb vinegars are great to have on hand for the perfect salad accompaniment. Use white or red vinegar and fresh herbs such as thyme, tarragon, dill, mint, oregano, chives, cilantro, basil, rosemary, or a combination. Chop fresh herbs to fill half of the bottle being used. In a saucepan, warm vinegar, and pour over the herbs. Cover the jar tightly, and place in a sunny window for 2 weeks, shaking daily. Strain vinegar, and taste. If the flavor is not strong enough, repeat the process. If the flavor is too strong, add a little more vinegar. When the desired flavor is achieved, bottle with a sprig of fresh herb, and seal. Herb vinegars keep for about 6 months.

HERB BUTTER

Herb butter is easy to make and adds a nice touch to any meal. It is delicious on fish, meat, vegetables, or bread. It may be easily shaped with molds or rolled in plastic wrap and sliced into rounds.

To make herb butter, add 1 tablespoon chopped fresh herbs to ½ cup slightly softened butter, the zest of ¼ lemon, ½ teaspoon lemon juice, and ¼ teaspoon Tabasco sauce. Pack carefully into rubber butter molds or tiny ice molds, and freeze for about 10 minutes. Remove from molds, and store in the freezer in a sealed container with waxed paper between the layers. Butter may also be rolled into a log and stored in the freezer, then sliced when needed. Place a small herb leaf flush on top of each slice for a special touch.

easy does it

Glass containers filled with peppers, oils, vinegars, and herbs are great table arrangements and make unique favors.

fireside *supper*

MENU 1

BAKED TURKEY
SANDWICHES ON
CINNAMON-RAISIN BREAD
WITH HORSERADISH
HONEY MUSTARD

WILD RICE TOSS WITH
SEASONAL FRUITS

PUMPKIN PARFAIT OR
PUMPKIN PIE CAKE

MENU 2

BEEF ROAST, POTATOES,
AND CARROTS

SEASONED BROCCOLI

ITALIAN
BROILED TOMATOES

BUTTERSCOTCH DELIGHT

BAKED TURKEY SANDWICHES ON CINNAMON-RAISIN BREAD

1 (5- or 6-pound) frozen turkey
  breast, thawed
Salt and pepper to taste
1 small onion, quartered
3 ribs celery
½ bell pepper, sliced
Cinnamon-raisin bread
Leaf lettuce

Preheat oven to 350 degrees. Line a pan with foil. Wash turkey, then season with salt and pepper. Place cut vegetables in neck cavity of turkey. Place turkey on foil in pan, breast side up, and bake for 1 hour, uncovered. Cover turkey with foil, and bake for 1 more hour (2 hours total cooking time). Let stand 15 minutes before removing foil. Slice, and serve on cinnamon-raisin bread with leaf lettuce and Horseradish Honey Mustard. Yield: 8-10 servings.

HORSERADISH HONEY MUSTARD:
½ cup honey mustard
1 tablespoon horseradish or to taste

Mix mustard and horseradish together well. Spread on sandwiches. Yield: 1½ cups.

Set a small tea table in front
of the fire, and enjoy a lingering
fireside dinner.

WILD RICE TOSS

1 cup long-grain and wild rice
Chicken broth
2 tablespoons butter, melted
½ cup green onions, finely chopped
½ cup almonds
1 (6-ounce) package dried cranberries

Cook rice according to package directions, omitting seasoning package if included, and substituting chicken broth for water. When cooked, toss with butter, onions, almonds, and cranberries. Yield: 6-8 servings.

PUMPKIN PARFAIT

2 (5-ounce) packages Pepperidge Farm Ginger Man
    Home Style Cookies
1 cup toasted pecan pieces, divided
3 tablespoons butter, melted
2 (3.4-ounce) packages instant butterscotch pudding
2 cups cold milk
½ (15-ounce) can pumpkin
1 large container whipped topping
1 teaspoon ground cinnamon

Crush cookies between waxed paper with a rolling pin; add ¾ cup pecans and melted butter. Mix, and set aside. Prepare butterscotch pudding with cold milk; place in refrigerator for 30 minutes. Remove from refrigerator; add pumpkin, and blend. To prepare parfaits, layer cookie mixture, pudding mixture, and whipped topping. Layer again, and end with a dollop of whipped topping sprinkled with cinnamon and remaining pecans. Yield: 8 servings.

PUMPKIN PIE CAKE

1 (15-ounce) can pumpkin
3 eggs, beaten
1 cup sugar
¼ teaspoon ground cloves
¼ teaspoon ground ginger
1½ teaspoons ground cinnamon
¼ teaspoon salt
1 (5-ounce) can evaporated milk
1 box butter-recipe yellow cake mix
1 cup pecans, chopped
1 stick butter, melted

Preheat oven to 350 degrees. Grease a 9 x 13-inch Pyrex dish with non-stick cooking spray, and set aside. Mix first 8 ingredients together with an electric mixer, and pour into prepared dish. In a separate bowl, combine cake mix and pecans, and sprinkle on pumpkin mixture. Drizzle with butter. Bake for 45 minutes, and serve with Flavored Whipped Cream. Yield: 12-16 servings.

FLAVORED WHIPPED CREAM:
¼ cup confectioner's sugar
½ pint whipping cream
Ground cinnamon for garnish

Beat together sugar and whipping cream, and sprinkle with cinnamon.

BEEF ROAST, POTATOES, AND CARROTS

1 (3- to 3½-pound) boneless chuck roast
¼ teaspoon salt
Meat tenderizer
⅓ cup canola oil
6 to 8 large red Irish potatoes, cut into wedges
8 ounces or more baby carrots
2 medium onions, cut into round slices
2 tablespoons margarine
Salt and pepper to taste

Wash roast, and sprinkle with salt and meat tenderizer. Heat oil in a large Dutch oven. Place roast in hot oil, and brown on all sides. Remove roast from oil; drain oil from Dutch oven. Put roast back in Dutch oven, and add enough water to cover roast. Cook roast on low heat for about three hours or until tender. Add potatoes, carrots, and onions, and cook until tender. Put pats of margarine on potatoes, carrots, and onions, and sprinkle with salt and pepper. Yield: 6-8 servings.

SEASONED BROCCOLI

1 bunch fresh broccoli
4 tablespoons butter, melted
1 teaspoon lemon pepper
1 teaspoon chives, chopped
Juice of ½ lemon or to taste

Steam broccoli until crisp-tender, and season with butter, lemon pepper, chives, and a little lemon juice. Yield: 4 servings.

ITALIAN BROILED TOMATOES

3 tablespoons butter, melted
3 tablespoons Italian breadcrumbs
2 tomatoes, halved
Grated parmesan cheese

Preheat oven to broil. Mix melted butter and breadcrumbs. Place on tomato tops, and cover with cheese. Broil to melt cheese. Yield: 4 servings.

Begin a tradition of drinking tea
and visiting before the fire.
Try different teas, and use special tea cups.
Discover scones, jams, and biscotti.

FEATHER YOUR NEST

Feathers make wonderful accents for fall arrangements. They are perfect with foliage, flowers, fruits, vegetables, cones, and many dried materials. Feathers are available at flower shops and craft stores in many lengths and colors.

You will need:

Feathers of assorted sizes and colors
Terracotta pot or decorative urn
Cascading ivy plant
Other natural materials as desired
Fresh flowers
Water picks

Add feathers to a simple pot of ivy with other dried materials, fall leaves, feather balls, lemons, pomegranates, sunflowers, cockscombs, and pepper berries for a stunning entryway arrangement. Arrange colorful flowers in water picks and greenery around the container to finish the look.

Placed in interesting containers, feathers can also become long-lasting focal points on mantels or sideboards or may be used as unique centerpieces.

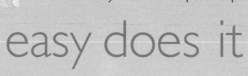

easy does it

Use natural cones, weeds, grasses, leaves, and berries with greenery in fall arrangements.
Feathers and stuffed birds bring a touch of nature to the table.

BUTTERSCOTCH DELIGHT

CRUST:

1 stick butter, softened
1 cup all-purpose flour
1 cup pecans, finely chopped

Preheat oven to 325 degrees. Mix softened butter with flour and pecans. Press into a 9 x 13-inch Pyrex baking dish. Bake for 20 minutes. Cool completely.

FILLING:

1 (8-ounce) package cream cheese,
  softened
1 cup confectioner's sugar
1 cup whipping topping

Combine all ingredients with a mixer. Pour over cooled Crust. Refrigerate until firm.

BUTTERSCOTCH:

2 (3.4-ounce) boxes instant butterscotch pudding
3 cups milk
1 teaspoon vanilla

Beat pudding and milk with mixer until thickened. Add vanilla. Pour over Filling.

TOPPING:

1½ cups whipped topping
1 jar commercial caramel sauce
1 cup pecans, chopped and toasted

Spread whipped topping over Butterscotch layer. When ready to serve, cut into squares, and drizzle with caramel sauce and pecans. Yield: 12-16 servings.

Pumpkin, butterscotch, and caramel flavors make great
fall desserts, sharing a delicious taste and a golden fall appearance.

harvest *dinner*

SPICY TOMATO SOUP

PORK MEDALLIONS WITH
MUSTARD CREAM SAUCE

SWEET POTATO MOLDS
WITH CRANBERRY SAUCE

SPINACH ROULADE

BEATEN BISCUITS

APPLESAUCE SPICE CAKE
WITH CANDIED PECANS

PUMPKIN BREAD WITH
SWEET CREAM SPREAD

CLASSIC
BUTTERSCOTCH PIE

CARAMEL SQUARES

SPICY TOMATO SOUP

4 tablespoons butter
1 bunch green onions, finely chopped
2 cans tomato soup
4 cans chicken broth
1 large can whole tomatoes, chopped
1 can Rotel diced tomatoes (You may
    omit and season soup with Tabasco
    sauce)
Pepper and basil to taste

Melt butter in a saucepan. Add green onions, and sauté until soft. Add tomato soup, chicken broth, chopped whole tomatoes, and Rotel tomatoes. Stir all ingredients together, and simmer for 30 minutes. Add Tabasco sauce if Rotel is omitted. Pepper and basil are good seasonings for this soup; add to taste. Yield: 10-12 servings.

Thanksgiving or harvest time is a wonderful time
to display an array of desserts on the sideboard
for family and friends to pick up after the meal
with coffee and tea in the late afternoon.

PORK MEDALLIONS WITH MUSTARD CREAM SAUCE

12 medallions of pork, ¾ to 1 inch thick
Salt and pepper to taste
Flour
4 tablespoons butter, divided
⅓ cup white wine
8 peppercorns, crushed
2 cups heavy cream
⅓ cup Dijon mustard
½ teaspoon salt
Parsley, chopped

Have the butcher cut 12 medallions 1 inch thick from a pork tenderloin or ¾ inch thick from a loin of pork. Flatten medallions between 2 sheets of waxed paper until they are ½ inch thick.

Sprinkle medallions with salt and pepper, and dust lightly with flour. In a skillet, sauté medallions in 3 tablespoons butter for 2 minutes on each side. Transfer to a platter, and keep warm.

Add to the skillet white wine and peppercorns, and boil this mixture, stirring in the brown bits that cling to the bottom and sides of the pan, until it is reduced by two-thirds.

Add heavy cream, and simmer the sauce mixture for 5 minutes or until it is slightly thickened. Remove pan from heat, and swirl in Dijon mustard and remaining 1 tablespoon butter cut into pieces.

Season sauce with ½ teaspoon salt, and pour over the pork. Sprinkle with chopped parsley. Yield: 12 servings.

Note: To cut calories, omit cream and substitute 2 cups of white wine that have been reduced until thickened.

Beverage glasses are placed
on the right at the tip of the knife.
Prepared beverages should
be presented and refilled from the right.

SWEET POTATO MOLDS WITH CRANBERRY SAUCE

1 pound sweet potatoes
2 eggs
¼ cup milk
1 tablespoon light brown sugar
½ teaspoon salt
½ teaspoon cinnamon

Bake sweet potatoes in a preheated 400-degree oven for 30-40 minutes or until tender; cool. Peel and cut into 1-inch pieces. Reduce oven temperature to 350 degrees. Purée potatoes in a food processor until smooth. Add remaining ingredients, and mix until combined.

Butter 6 ramekins, and fill with mixture. Place ramekins in a water bath, and cover loosely with foil. Bake for about 45 minutes or until a knife inserted in center comes out clean. Cool for 10 minutes, and unmold. Yield: 6.

CRANBERRY SAUCE:
1 (8-ounce) can cranberry sauce
¼ cup water
2 teaspoons lemon juice

Process all ingredients in a food processor until thick and smooth, about 2 minutes. Heat sauce until warm, and pour over sweet potato molds.

SPINACH ROULADE

A roulade, or fallen soufflé, is cooked in a jelly-roll pan, turned out, and rolled up.
Breadcrumbs
3 packages frozen chopped spinach, thawed and
*   squeezed dry*
Salt and freshly ground pepper to taste
Pinch nutmeg
6 tablespoons melted butter
4 eggs, separated
4 tablespoons parmesan cheese

Butter a 10 x 15-inch pan, and line with waxed paper. Butter the waxed paper, and sprinkle with breadcrumbs. In a bowl, combine spinach, salt, pepper, nutmeg, and melted butter. Add egg yolks, 1 at a time, beating well after each one.

In a separate bowl, beat egg whites until they hold a peak as for a soufflé. Fold ¼ of the whites into the spinach, then add spinach mixture to the whites. Pour into the prepared pan. Smooth the top evenly with a rubber spatula. Sprinkle grated parmesan cheese over top of mixture.

Bake in a preheated 350-degree oven for 12-16 minutes or until center feels barely firm when touched. When done, place a piece of aluminum foil over the top, and invert the pan. Peel off waxed paper, and discard. Use the foil to help roll the spinach into a cylinder. Slice into rounds to serve, and sprinkle with extra parmesan cheese, if desired. Yield: 10 servings.

BEATEN BISCUITS

2 cups unbleached flour
1 teaspoon salt
1 stick butter, cut into pieces
½ cup ice water

Preheat oven to 350 degrees. In a food processor, mix together flour and salt. Add butter, and process until mixture is like cornmeal. With the machine running, add ice water through the tube in a slow stream. Process for 2 minutes.

Remove dough; roll out on a floured surface to a thickness of ⅛ inch, and fold in half to form two layers. Cut with a round cookie cutter, and prick with the tines of a fork twice in the center of each biscuit.

Place on an ungreased cookie sheet, and bake for 25-30 minutes. Remove from oven, and test a biscuit by splitting to see if the center is doughy. If so, place back in the oven for a few more minutes.

PUMPKIN DISPLAYS

Use pumpkins as containers without cutting them so they will last longer. Secure floral foam in a green container on top with florist tape. Next, cover the mechanics with fruit, berries, and fall foliage. Pull apart a grapevine wreath, and weave it around the pumpkin containers, or weave it around the pumpkins alone.

For table decorations, top small clay pots with green sheet moss, tiny pumpkins with pieces of floral foam on top, and small bunches of fall flowers and berries. Swirl delicate vines around the pumpkins.

easy does it

APPLESAUCE SPICE CAKE WITH CANDIED PECANS

1 cup unsalted butter, at room temperature
2 cups sugar, divided
3 eggs or ¾ cup Egg Beaters
3 cups all-purpose flour
1 teaspoon ground nutmeg
1 tablespoon ground cinnamon
1 teaspoon ground cloves
½ teaspoon ground cardamom
½ teaspoon salt
2 teaspoons baking powder
2 cups unsweetened applesauce
2 teaspoons real vanilla extract
1 cup pecan pieces, lightly toasted
2 cups apples, peeled and chopped

Preheat oven to 350 degrees. Butter a 10-inch spring-form pan; dust with ¼ cup sugar. Beat remaining butter and sugar for about 5 minutes until light and fluffy. Beat in eggs, 1 at a time. In another bowl, sift together flour, spices, salt, and baking powder. On slow speed, alternate adding flour mixture and applesauce to butter mixture until well-combined. Add vanilla; mix well. Stir in nuts and apple by hand. Pour into pan. Bake for 1 hour and 45-50 minutes or until tester comes out clean. Cool on rack. Brush top of cooled cake with Glaze. Arrange Candied Pecans on top. Yield: 10-12 servings.

GLAZE:

1 cup unsweetened apple juice
¼ cup brown sugar

In a small pan over medium heat, simmer juice and sugar until thickened and reduced by at least half.

CANDIED PECANS:

½ cup pecan halves
2 teaspoons butter, melted
½ cup sugar

Toast pecan halves in oven for 5 minutes. Immediately toss with butter, then with sugar. Let cool in pan.

PUMPKIN BREAD WITH SWEET CREAM SPREAD

1½ cups sugar
2 eggs
½ (15-ounce) can pumpkin
⅓ cup water
½ cup oil
1¾ cups flour
1½ teaspoons soda
¾ teaspoon salt
½ teaspoon nutmeg
½ teaspoon cinnamon, plus more for garnish
½ cup nuts, chopped

Preheat oven to 350 degrees. Mix all ingredients in the order listed. Bake for 1 hour in greased and floured 3 x 5-inch loaf pans. Top with Sweet Cream Spread and cinnamon, and serve with Spicy Pumpkin Butter. Yield: 2.

SWEET CREAM SPREAD:

3 ounces cream cheese
2 tablespoons confectioner's sugar

Beat ingredients together until well-combined.

SPICY PUMPKIN BUTTER:

¼ cup dark brown sugar, firmly packed
2 tablespoons sugar
¼ cup water
¼ teaspoon ground allspice
⅛ teaspoon ground ginger
¼ teaspoon ground cloves
¼ teaspoon ground nutmeg
½ teaspoon ground cinnamon
1½ cups pumpkin

Combine sugars, water, and spices in a large glass measuring cup. Microwave on high for 3 minutes; stir. Add pumpkin, and microwave on high for 5 minutes. Let cool, then refrigerate. Keeps several weeks in refrigerator or can be frozen. Yield: 2 cups.

Beautiful pumpkins, gourds, fruits, vegetables, dried materials, and flowers in subdued colors will enhance any autumn dessert display.

FRUIT AND VEGETABLE TURKEY

Combine fresh fruits and vegetables to fashion a turkey for a holiday display.

You will need:

Large platter
2 blocks floral foam
1 large pineapple with full, pretty greenery
2 bananas
2 small pears
2 small apples
1 yellow squash with good crook and small green stem in place
Toothpicks
2 whole cloves
Fresh boxwood or greenery that has been conditioned by soaking in water for several hours and then refrigerated in a plastic bag
Several stems button mums

Stack floral foam on a large platter. Round the corners with a knife, and place the removed pieces on each end of the platter. Secure them with toothpicks, forming a large oval as a base for the turkey body. Carve out a small indention in the top of the base to create a place for the large part of the pineapple to rest. Attach bananas with toothpicks to the sides of the pineapple for turkey wings. Place one pear and one apple below the banana to complete the wing. The pear creates the drumstick. Attach the squash for the neck and head with a toothpick. Add cloves for eyes, and arrange the boxwood and mums around the base. The turkey will last for 4 or 5 days.

easy does it

CLASSIC BUTTERSCOTCH PIE

PIE CRUST:
1 Pillsbury refrigerated pie crust
Graham cracker crumbs

Lightly roll out pie crust, using graham cracker crumbs on the rolling surface instead of flour. Use some crumbs on the bottom and top of pastry. Place in a pie pan, and crimp the edges. Refrigerate dough for 30 minutes. Prick dough all around with a fork.

Double-fold aluminum foil, and press into pie shell. Prick with a fork through the foil. Place pie shell in freezer while the oven preheats to 375 degrees. Bake for 15 minutes. Remove foil. Bake for 10-15 minutes more.

FILLING:
¼ cup cornstarch
¼ teaspoon salt
½ cup evaporated milk
5 egg yolks
6 tablespoons butter
1 cup light brown sugar
2 cups milk
1 teaspoon vanilla
1 cup cream
2 teaspoons sugar
Toffee bits

Dissolve cornstarch and salt in evaporated milk. Beat in egg yolks, and set aside. Place butter and brown sugar in a saucepan, and bring to a boil. Boil until temperature reaches 220 degrees on a candy thermometer. Slowly add milk, and stir until mixture returns to a boil. Boil for 1 minute, then add vanilla. Immediately pour hot filling into a shallow pan; cover with plastic wrap. Cool for 30 minutes. Pour 1 tablespoon of filling into yolk mixture, and combine. Add yolk mixture back to filling, and combine. Pour warm filling into baked Pie Crust. Refrigerate for 2-3 hours. Whip cream to soft peaks, then add sugar; beat until barely stiff. Spread over filling; top with toffee bits and White Chocolate Butterflies. Yield: 6-8 servings.

WHITE CHOCOLATE BUTTERFLIES:

Draw butterfly wing shapes on paper, and place parchment over drawings. Heat white chocolate in a glass bowl in the microwave on low until melted. Pipe melted white chocolate over drawings, and let dry. Place two wings together to resemble a butterfly lighting into the whipped cream.

CARAMEL SQUARES

1 stick butter
1 cup brown sugar
1 egg
1 cup all-purpose flour, sifted
1 teaspoon baking powder
Pinch salt
1 teaspoon vanilla
1⅓ cups walnuts, chopped

Preheat oven to 350 degrees. Grease a 9-inch square pan. Combine butter and sugar in a saucepan, and stir over medium heat until very smooth. Cool. Add unbeaten egg. Sift in flour, baking powder, and salt; add vanilla. Stir in walnuts. Mix well until smooth. Bake for 30 minutes. Cool before cutting into squares. Frost with Caramel Frosting. Yield: about 2 dozen.

CARAMEL FROSTING:
3¼ cups sugar, divided
¾ cup milk
1 stick butter
6 marshmallows
1 teaspoon vanilla

Brown ¾ cup sugar in a skillet, stirring constantly until caramelized. Place remaining 2½ cups sugar and milk in a saucepan, and bring to a boil. Boil for 3 minutes. Add caramelized sugar, and boil for 3 minutes. Add butter, marshmallows, and vanilla; stir until melted. Beat until thick and ready to spread.

For appealing food presentation,
layer plates of different patterns and styles.

Pork Tenderloin
Souffle with Chicken
Yellow Squash stuffed with Spinach
Madeline
Hot Spiced Apricots
Rolls

Winter

Boxes from the attic appear with glistening treasures
to dance on tree branches among tiny white twinkling lights.
It is the spirit of the season to dress
doorways in evergreen wreaths and
garlands of berries and bows to welcome guests.
It is a time of happy children
decorating sugar cookies in the kitchen.
Winter brings Christmas, a birthday to celebrate
with loved ones and a special time for memories and miracles.

holiday *tea* party

SESAME ASPARAGUS
ROLL-UPS

APPLE-CINNAMON
SANDWICHES

STRIPED HAM SANDWICHES

SPINACH SQUARES

CREAM SCONES
WITH JAM AND MOCK
DEVONSHIRE CREAM

BANANA NUT BREAD
STARS WITH CREAM
CHEESE FROSTING

ALMOND EGGNOG
BABY BUNDT CAKES

PECAN PIE MUFFINS

LEMON SQUARES

TARTLETS WITH FILLINGS

CHRISTMAS PUNCH

SESAME ASPARAGUS ROLL-UPS

12 fresh asparagus spears
12 slices white bread, with crusts removed
½ cup blue cheese, crumbled
1 (8-ounce) package cream cheese, softened
1 stick butter, melted
1 tablespoon sesame seeds

Preheat oven to 375 degrees. Trim each asparagus spear to 6 inches long. Flatten bread between waxed paper with a rolling pin. Mix blue cheese and cream cheese together, and spread on bread. Place an asparagus spear on each piece of bread; roll up, and press ends down. Dip each sandwich in melted butter. Place on an ungreased baking sheet, and sprinkle with sesame seeds. Bake for 15 minutes or until golden. Yield: 12.

To **set the mood** for the party, send out invitations shaped like tea cups or teapots; you might even want to attach real tea bags.

APPLE-CINNAMON SANDWICHES

1 (8-ounce) package cream cheese, softened
2 tablespoons brown sugar
½ teaspoon cinnamon
¼ teaspoon nutmeg
1 teaspoon vanilla
2 red or Golden Delicious apples, unpeeled
Lemon juice
1 loaf cinnamon-raisin bread
⅓ cup walnuts, finely chopped and toasted

Combine cream cheese, brown sugar, cinnamon, nutmeg, and vanilla. Beat with an electric mixer on medium speed for 1 minute or until smooth. Set aside. Core apples, and cut into thin horizontal slices. Brush with lemon juice. To assemble each sandwich, spread one side of two slices of bread with cream cheese mixture. Top one slice of bread with apple slices, then place the other slice of bread on top of apples, cream cheese side down. Trim edges. Cut diagonally twice. Lightly spread cream cheese mixture on front edges. Dip into chopped walnuts, and arrange on tray. Yield: about 16.

STRIPED HAM SANDWICHES

3 ounces sliced cooked ham
4 teaspoons mayonnaise
½ teaspoon Dijon mustard
¼ cup cream cheese, softened
4 teaspoons fresh chives, chopped
Salt and pepper to taste
½ cup plus 1 tablespoon butter, softened
Wheat bread
White bread
Fresh chives for garnish

Mix ham, mayonnaise, and mustard in a food processor until well-blended. Mix together cream cheese, chives, salt, and pepper. To assemble each sandwich, butter 2 slices of wheat bread on one side and 1 slice of white bread on both sides. Spread half of ham mixture on one slice of buttered wheat bread. Cover with white bread. Spread cream cheese mixture over white bread, and cover with wheat bread. Remove crusts from bread. Cut each sandwich into fingers. Arrange on serving plate, and garnish with chives. Yield: about 12.

TEA CUP WREATH

Hang this wreath year-round to display an heirloom collection of cups.

You will need:
Large oval grapevine wreath
Green florist wire
Teapot (this is a wire one painted gold)
Small cups and spoons
Various ribbons and gold braids
Preserved lemon leaves
Quick Grab clear glue

Wire the teapot to the top or bottom of the grapevine wreath. Choose favorite small cups to hang by their handles from gold ribbon or cord in different lengths. Attach other cups and spoons evenly around wreath with wire, and accent with bows, ribbons, and cords. Insert lemon leaves randomly into the grapevines, and glue into place.

easy does it

SPINACH SQUARES

2 (10-ounce) packages frozen chopped spinach, thawed
2 tablespoons onion, finely chopped
3 tablespoons butter
4 eggs, beaten
⅓ cup breadcrumbs
1 (10½-ounce) can cream of mushroom soup
⅓ cup parmesan cheese, finely grated
⅛ teaspoon white pepper
¼ teaspoon oregano
1 small can chopped mushrooms, drained
Saltine crackers

Preheat oven to 350 degrees. Drain spinach, and press out all water possible. Sauté onion in butter until soft; set aside. Combine eggs, breadcrumbs, soup, cheese, seasonings, and spinach. Blend in onions and mushrooms. Pour into a greased 9 x 13-inch Pyrex dish. Bake for 30-35 minutes. Cut into small squares, and place on crackers. Yield: 20 servings.

CREAM SCONES WITH JAM AND MOCK DEVONSHIRE CREAM

2 cups all-purpose flour
2½ teaspoons baking powder
¼ teaspoon salt
¼ cup sugar
4 tablespoons butter
¾ cup whipping cream

Preheat oven to 400 degrees. Sift together flour, baking powder, and salt; add sugar. Cut in butter until crumbly. Add cream, and blend well. Dough will be sticky. Flour a flat workspace, and knead dough for about 30 seconds. Roll out to ½ inch thick, and cut to shape of your choice. Bake for 15 minutes. Serve with Raspberry or Strawberry Jam and Mock Devonshire Cream. Yield: about 12.

RASPBERRY OR STRAWBERRY JAM:
2 quarts fully ripe raspberries or strawberries
1 (1¾-ounce) box Sure-Jell fruit pectin
7 cups sugar

Wash and stem berries. Crush, 1 layer at a time, to let juice flow freely. Measure 4½ cups berries into saucepan; mix in Sure-Jell. Place over high heat, and stir until mixture reaches a hard boil. Add sugar all at once; mix well. Bring to a full rolling boil for 1 minute, stirring constantly. Remove from heat; skim off foam with metal spoon. Stir and skim for 5 minutes to cool slightly and prevent floating fruit. Quickly ladle into sterilized jars, and seal at once. Yield: about 8½ pints.

MOCK DEVONSHIRE CREAM:
2 cups sour cream
2 tablespoons confectioner's sugar
1 teaspoon vanilla extract

Mix together all ingredients. Yield: about 2 cups.

VARIATION:
½ cup cream cheese, softened
2 tablespoons confectioner's sugar
½ cup sour cream

Mix together all ingredients. Yield: about 1 cup.

BANANA NUT BREAD STARS WITH CREAM CHEESE FROSTING

1 cup (about 2 to 3) ripe bananas
1 egg
¾ cup milk
3 tablespoons cooking oil
3½ teaspoons baking powder
½ teaspoon salt
1 cup sugar
2½ cups all-purpose flour
1 cup walnuts, chopped
1 (16-ounce) can cream cheese frosting

Preheat oven to 350 degrees. Grease a 9 x 5-inch loaf pan with non-stick cooking spray. Purée peeled bananas. Add other ingredients, mixing well after each addition. Pour into pan, and bake for 50 minutes or until toothpick comes out clean. Remove from pan, and cool on wire rack. To serve, cut slices into star shapes, and frost.

Ornaments are the perfect favors for any holiday party, as are tea cup or teapot shaped sugar cookies wrapped in cellophane bags with bows.

TEA CUP CHRISTMAS TREE

Adorn a small artificial tree with heirloom teacups, silver spoons, tea napkins, and bows.

You will need:
Small artificial tree
Green florist wire
Small teapot
Tea cups (Demitasse or small cups work well)
Silver spoons
Lots of different ribbons
Gold braid
Fresh greenery (Seeded eucalyptus and lemon
  leaves work well and dry nicely)
Water picks

Wire the teapot onto the top of the tree, and wire cups, spoons, and accessories onto the tree's limbs. Bend the wire branches to aid in holding cups in position. Then tie bows and gold braids among the cups. Place the greenery in water picks, and distribute it among the branches, bending branches when necessary.

Have guests wear vintage hats or even vintage clothes and jewelry for a fun atmosphere.

ANTIQUE PLATE TIERED SERVER

Using vintage china and candlesticks, make a tiered server for your tea table or as a gift for a tea-loving friend .

You will need:
Vintage plates of various sizes (dinner, breakfast, dessert, bread and butter)
Candlesticks or holders of various heights
Quick Grab clear glue

Glue plates of pleasing patterns onto candlesticks, placing the largest on the bottom and the smallest on the top.

easy does it

ALMOND EGGNOG BABY BUNDT CAKES

1 cup sliced almonds
1 box yellow cake mix
1½ cups eggnog
2 eggs
1 teaspoon rum extract
⅛ teaspoon ground nutmeg
4 tablespoons butter, melted

Preheat oven to 350 degrees. Grease cupcake bundt pans with non-stick cooking spray. Press almonds onto the bottoms and sides of bundtlettes; set aside. In a large mixing bowl, beat cake mix, eggnog, eggs, rum extract, nutmeg, and melted butter on low speed for 30 seconds or just until moistened. Beat on medium for 2 minutes until smooth. Pour into prepared pans. Bake for about 12 minutes. Cool slightly before removing from pans to a wire rack. Yield: 24.

PECAN PIE MUFFINS

1 cup pecans, chopped
1 cup brown sugar, firmly packed
½ cup all-purpose flour
2 eggs
½ cup butter, melted

Preheat oven to 350 degrees. Combine first 3 ingredients in a large bowl; set aside. Beat eggs until foamy. Add butter to eggs, then add to dry ingredients, stirring just until moistened. Spray miniature muffin pans with non-stick cooking spray; spoon batter into cups, filling each cup ⅔ full. Bake for 14-16 minutes. Remove from pans immediately, and cool on wire racks. Yield: 24.

LEMON SQUARES

CRUST:

½ pound unsalted butter, at room temperature
½ cup sugar
2 cups all-purpose flour
⅛ teaspoon kosher salt

Cream butter and sugar until light in the bowl of an electric mixer fitted with the paddle attachment. Combine flour and salt; with the mixer on low, add to butter until just mixed. Dump dough onto a well-floured board, and gather into a ball. Flatten dough with floured hands, and press it into a 9 x 13-inch baking dish, building up a ½-inch edge on all sides. Chill. Preheat oven to 350 degrees; bake crust for 15-20 minutes or until very lightly browned. Let cool on wire rack. Leave the oven on.

FILLING:

6 large eggs, at room temperature
3 cups sugar
2 tablespoons lemon zest (4 to 6 lemons)
1 cup freshly squeezed lemon juice
1 cup all-purpose flour
Confectioner's sugar for dusting

Whisk together eggs, sugar, lemon zest, lemon juice, and flour. Pour over crust, and bake for 30-35 minutes or until filling is set. Let cool to room temperature. Cut into squares, and dust with confectioner's sugar. Yield: 24 servings.

A tea party can
be a nice rest
from a day of Christmas shopping.

TARTLETS WITH FILLINGS

PASTRY:

⅓ cup sugar
2 cups all-purpose flour, unsifted
2 sticks butter, cut into 16 pieces
1 egg
1 teaspoon vanilla
Whipped topping
Chocolate shavings and toasted nuts for garnish

Cream sugar and flour in food processor with butter. Pulse until mixture resembles grains of rice. Mix egg and vanilla in a separate bowl, then pour through food processor tube and pulse. Chill for 1 hour in bowl covered with plastic wrap. Press into small tart tins. Bake in a preheated 350-degree oven for about 5 minutes, depending on shell sizes. Fill with Lemon Filling or with instant chocolate pudding, butterscotch pudding, or coconut pudding. Top with whipped topping; garnish with chocolate shavings and toasted nuts. Yield: 24.

LEMON FILLING:

3 egg yolks
1 can sweetened condensed milk
½ cup lemon juice

Beat egg yolks. Mix in condensed milk and lemon juice, and beat well until creamy. Fill pastry shells.

CHRISTMAS PUNCH

7 cups water
1½ cups sugar
3 heaping tablespoons Red Hots cinnamon candy
1 quart cranberry juice
3 cups orange juice
⅛ cup plus 3 tablespoons lemon juice concentrate

Pour water into a large Dutch oven, and bring to a boil. Add sugar and Red Hots; stir until dissolved. Pour in juices; simmer. Cool, and refrigerate. To serve, heat until hot. Yield: about 1 gallon.

christmas *dinner* party

MENU 1

GRILLED PORK
TENDERLOIN

SHRIMP, CHICKEN, AND
ARTICHOKE CASSEROLE
OVER CHEESE SOUFFLÉ

YELLOW SQUASH STUFFED
WITH SPINACH

HOT SPICED APRICOTS

COCONUT CHEESECAKE

MENU 2

ROLLED CHICKEN
BREASTS OVER RICE

SPECIAL GREEN BEANS

FROZEN CRANBERRY SALAD

POACHED PEARS
WITH CARAMEL SAUCE

GRILLED PORK TENDERLOIN

1 (2- to 3-pound) pork tenderloin
Dijon mustard
Brown sugar

Rinse pork, and pat dry with paper towels. Spread Dijon mustard over meat, then coat with brown sugar. Grill for about 30 minutes or until pork is cooked through and reaches an internal temperature of 170 degrees on a meat thermometer. Slice; serve with Dijon mustard.

SHRIMP, CHICKEN, AND ARTICHOKE CASSEROLE OVER CHEESE SOUFFLÉ

2 (14-ounce) cans artichoke hearts, drained
4 boneless, skinless chicken breasts, boiled and
*   chopped into bite-sized pieces*
2 pounds shrimp, steamed, peeled, and deveined
1 pound fresh mushrooms, sliced
¼ cup butter, melted
3 tablespoons flour
1 cup milk
1½ cups chicken broth
⅓ cup sherry
1 tablespoon worcestershire sauce
Salt and pepper to taste
1 sleeve saltine crackers, crushed
Paprika to taste
¼ cup butter, melted

Make a menu card for each table
in the style of your invitations.
Embellish with a bow or special decoration,
and place it on an easel on each table.

Preheat oven to 375 degrees. Arrange artichoke hearts in the bottom of a greased casserole dish. Add chicken and shrimp. Sauté mushrooms in butter. Sprinkle flour over mushrooms; stir until blended. Gradually add milk, then blend in chicken broth and sherry. Add worcestershire sauce, salt, and pepper, stirring constantly. Simmer for about 5 minutes, and pour over chicken and shrimp. Combine crushed crackers, paprika, and melted butter, and sprinkle over casserole. Bake for 40 minutes. Serve over Cheese Soufflé. Yield: 10 servings.

CHEESE SOUFFLÉ:

6 tablespoons butter
6 tablespoons flour
½ teaspoon salt
½ teaspoon paprika
Cayenne pepper, onion salt, dry mustard, and
*   worcestershire sauce to taste*
1½ cups milk
12 ounces sharp cheddar cheese, grated
6 large cold eggs, separated

Butter a 2-quart soufflé dish. In a double boiler, melt butter, and blend in flour and seasonings. Add milk, and cook, stirring constantly, until smooth and thickened. Add cheese; stir until melted. Remove from stove. Beat egg yolks with a mixer until thick and lemon-colored. Gradually stir yolks into cheese mixture by adding 1 tablespoon of hot mixture to yolks, then adding yolk mixture back to hot mixture. With a clean, dry mixer, beat egg whites until very stiff but not dry. Slowly pour cheese mixture into whites, folding carefully with a rubber spatula until well-blended and no large lumps of white remain. Bake, uncovered, in a preheated 350-degree oven for 45 minutes or until puffed and golden brown. Do not open oven door until time is up. Yield: 10 servings.

Gilded fruit and vegetable ornaments make great table decorations when **combined** with seasonal greenery or in place settings on napkins or as unique placecards.

YELLOW SQUASH STUFFED WITH SPINACH

2 (10-ounce) packages frozen chopped spinach
4 tablespoons butter
2 tablespoons flour
2 tablespoons onion, chopped
½ cup evaporated milk
½ teaspoon black pepper
½ teaspoon celery salt
¾ teaspoon garlic salt
1 teaspoon worcestershire sauce
Red pepper to taste
¼ cup jalapeños, drained and chopped
6 ounces Velveeta processed cheese,
   cut into small pieces
6 yellow squash
1 teaspoon salt
½ stick margarine, melted
1 sleeve saltine crackers, crushed

Cook spinach according to package directions; drain but reserve ½ cup liquid. Melt butter in saucepan over low heat; stir in flour until blended and smooth, but not brown. Add onion, and cook until soft. Combine spinach liquid and evaporated milk. Add slowly to flour mixture, stirring constantly to avoid lumps. Cook, stirring, until smooth and thick. Stir in seasonings, jalapeños, and cheese until melted. Combine with cooked spinach. Boil squash in a saucepan with salt until squash is easily pierced with a fork. Cool; split lengthwise, and scoop out pulp. Stuff shells with spinach mixture. For topping, mix melted margarine with crushed crackers; sprinkle on top. Bake in a preheated 350-degree oven for 30 minutes. Yield: 12.

HOT SPICED APRICOTS

2 large cans peeled apricots
2 boxes light brown sugar
1 large box Ritz crackers, crumbled
1½ sticks butter, cut into pats

Preheat oven to 300 degrees. Drain apricots, and place in a greased 9 x 13-inch Pyrex dish. Top with brown sugar, crumbled Ritz crackers, and pats of butter. Bake for 1 hour. Yield: 10-12 servings.

COCONUT CHEESECAKE

CRUST:

1 cup flaked coconut, toasted
¾ cup pecans, ground
2 tablespoons butter, melted

Preheat oven to 350 degrees. Combine coconut, ground pecans, and melted butter. Press mixture onto the bottom of a 9-inch springform pan. Set aside.

FILLING:

3 (8-ounce) packages cream cheese, softened
½ cup sugar
½ teaspoon vanilla
¼ teaspoon almond extract
3 eggs

Beat together cream cheese, sugar, vanilla, and almond extract in a large mixing bowl with an electric mixer on low speed until smooth. Add eggs all at once. Beat on low speed until just combined; do not overbeat. Pour over crust, and bake for 35 minutes. Set aside.

TOPPING:

1 egg white
½ teaspoon vanilla
⅓ cup sugar
⅔ cup flaked coconut, toasted
Toasted coconut for garnish

Beat egg white, vanilla, and sugar in a small bowl with an electric mixer until soft peaks form. Fold in coconut. Spread on cheesecake. Return to oven, and bake for 20 minutes more. Cool on wire rack for 15 minutes. Loosen sides of cheesecake by running a knife along inside edge of pan. Remove sides of pan. Cool for 1 hour. Cover, and chill for at least 4 hours before serving. Garnish with additional toasted coconut. Yield: 10-12 servings.

ROLLED CHICKEN BREASTS

1 (2.25-ounce) jar sliced dried beef
6 boneless, skinless chicken breasts
White pepper, paprika, onion salt, and celery salt
   to taste
12 strips bacon
2 cans cream of mushroom soup
1 cup sour cream
1 (8-ounce) package cream cheese, softened
Cooked rice

Preheat oven to 325 degrees. Grease a 9 x 13-inch pan with non-stick cooking spray. Spread sliced dried beef on the bottom of the pan in a single layer. Cut each chicken breast into 2 small strips. Sprinkle each strip with pepper, paprika, onion salt, and celery salt. Fold each strip into a roll with spices on inside; wrap a piece of bacon on the outside, and secure with a toothpick. Place each chicken roll on top of a piece of dried beef.

Combine soup, sour cream, and cream cheese, and pour over chicken breasts. Cover with foil, and bake for 2 hours. Remove foil, and brown. Serve over rice. Yield: 8-10 servings.

Planning and organization
are especially important during the holiday season.
Plan meals around dishes that can be prepared ahead, served easily,
and beautifully displayed.

SPECIAL GREEN BEANS

4 strips bacon
½ medium onion, chopped
1 cup slivered almonds
3 (16-ounce) cans Allen's cut green beans
½ cup vinegar
⅓ cup sugar

In a large saucepan, cook bacon until crisp. Remove bacon, crumble, and set aside. Sauté onion in bacon drippings. Mix bacon, onion, almonds, and green beans. Add vinegar and sugar. Simmer for 30-40 minutes. Beans can be refrigerated at this point. Bake in a 9 x 13-inch dish in a preheated 300-degree oven for 1½ hours. Yield: 8-10 servings.

FROZEN CRANBERRY SALAD

1 (8-ounce) package cream cheese, softened
2 tablespoons mayonnaise
2 tablespoons sugar
1 (16-ounce) can whole berry cranberry sauce
1 (8-ounce) can crushed pineapple, drained
½ cup pecans, chopped
1 (8-ounce) container whipped topping
½ cup confectioner's sugar, sifted
1 teaspoon vanilla extract

Combine cream cheese, mayonnaise, and sugar. Add cranberries, pineapple, and pecans, and set aside. Combine whipped topping, confectioner's sugar, and vanilla, and beat well. Fold whipped topping mixture into cream cheese mixture. Spoon into lined muffin tins, and freeze. Yield: about 24.

POACHED PEARS WITH CARAMEL SAUCE

2 cups water
¾ cup sugar
4 Bosc pears, peeled, halved, and cored
Vanilla ice cream
Commercial chocolate sauce
Toasted pistachio nuts for garnish

In a medium saucepan, bring water and sugar to a simmer over medium heat, stirring until sugar dissolves; remove from heat. Place pear halves in saucepan with sugar syrup immediately after peeling to prevent discoloration. Poach pears over low heat just below simmer until tender when pierced with a sharp knife, about 10 minutes. Remove from heat, and let pears cool in syrup. Remove pears with a slotted spoon, and set aside.

To assemble dessert, put a tablespoon of Caramel Sauce on plate. Place pear half on plate with a scoop of ice cream. Drizzle with chocolate sauce, and sprinkle with toasted pistachio nuts. Yield: about 8 servings.

CARAMEL SAUCE:
2 cups dark cane syrup
⅓ cup sugar
⅓ cup boiling water

Combine ingredients in a saucepan, and heat until mixture comes to a boil. Remove from heat.

Share leftover party food
with sick friends,
the elderly, or a shelter.

EASY CHRISTMAS WREATH

Create a fresh Christmas wreath by enhancing an artificial green wreath with fresh greenery such as magnolia, pine, cedar, and holly. Hot glue greenery to the wreath, then add a bow, fruit, or flowers. The wreath will last outside the entire month unless it is in full sun.

To hang wreath on the door, place a tiny flat-headed nail or tack in the top center of door. Hang wreath with a loop of sturdy fishing line.

Garlands can be made in the same fashion. Or instead of traditional greenery, use smilax around doorways. After conditioning for at least 24 hours in water, it will remain fresh in cool climates for about 2 weeks.

PICTURE ORNAMENTS

Enjoy special memories over and over by using treasured photographs to create beautiful ornaments. For an antique appearance, reproduce the pictures in black and white or sepia tone. These also make wonderful gifts or tags for packages.

You will need:
Photographs of your choice (Photo Christmas cards work well)
Small pieces of glass or Plexiglass, no larger than 4 x 4 inches or 3 x 5 inches (available at frame and craft stores)
Scissors
Paper for backing
Double-stick tape
Black fine-line permanent marker
Ribbons and braids
Small brass or silver rings (available at craft stores)
Various beads and charms (available at craft stores)
Small pliers and wire cutters
Self-adhesive lead tape (available from Van Dykes Restorers, www.vandykes.com or 800/787-3355)
J-B Weld (available at hardware stores)

Decide the glass shape that is best for your picture. Trace picture and paper backing to the exact size of the glass, and cut to fit. Use double-stick tape to secure the picture to the backing. Write name and date on backing with permanent marker. Sandwich glass, picture, and backing together.

For braid-trim ornaments, place a small amount of hot glue on a 12- to 16-inch strip of gold braid. Beginning at the top of the ornament, carefully guide the braid around the edges, pressing braid to the front and back of the glass to create a frame. Insert small brass rings into braid at the top for ribbon hangers, and insert a ring at the bottom for hanging beads and charms. Attach ribbons for hanging.

For leaded glass ornaments, gently press edges of self-adhesive lead tape to form a U shape. Remove backing paper. For curved glass shapes, begin at the top of the ornament and press lead around the edges of glass. For rectangular and square shapes, miter corners of lead tape by cutting four strips the lengths of the sides of your glass, then cutting ends of each piece to form a V shape. Press strips onto edges of glass. Seal edges with J-B Weld, mixed according to package directions. Use J-B Weld to attach silver rings for ribbon hangers to the top of the frame and a ring to the bottom to attach beads and charms. Allow to dry, then attach ribbons for hanging. Attach beads and charms.

Decorate your home with plants such as orchids, paperwhites, **poinsettias**, ivy, and amaryllis that will last **throughout** the month.

GINGERBREAD SPICE ORNAMENTS

You will need:

8 ounces applesauce
2 (2.47-ounce) bottles powdered cinnamon
Rubber gloves
Rolling pin
Waxed paper
Small or medium cookie cutters
Plastic drinking straw
Red and white dimensional paint
Cake-decorating small silver balls
Clear glitter
Ribbons and cords

Mix applesauce and all of the cinnamon except about 1 tablespoon reserved to sprinkle on rolling surface or rolling pin to prevent sticking. Knead with your hands, wearing rubber gloves, until pliable and a good dough consistency. Roll out between two sheets of waxed paper to about ⅛ inch thick, and cut out with cookie cutters. Punch a hole in each cookie ornament with the straw. Place on a flat surface on waxed paper, and allow to dry for 2-3 days. Decorate with dimensional paint and silver balls, and sprinkle with clear glitter. Allow to dry for about 8 hours, then run ribbon or cord through holes for hanging. Yield: 18-20.

NATURAL SPICE ORNAMENTS

Create spice ornaments by hot-gluing whole cinnamon sticks, star anise, whole nutmegs, whole allspice, tiny cones, and leaves to dried fruit with ribbons and balls. You may want to add a drop of scented oil to enhance the spicy aroma.

Decorate **early** so you and your family can begin enjoying the holidays.

Try to have presents bought and wrapped **prior to** December. Special handmade ornaments make lovely hostess gifts and are great tied on top of packages.

PRETTY PACKAGES

Elegant handmade gift packages tell the recipients how special they are to you.

You will need:

Boxes
Prepasted wallpaper
Scissors
White poster board
Hole punch
Pencil
Ruler
Ribbon
Gold broad-line marking pen

For boxes with removable lids, draw the exterior box size and lid size on the back of wallpaper. Cut out coverings with as few seams as possible. Wet wallpaper, and cover the box and its lid separately, folding edges inside. Allow to dry overnight, then add ribbons, bows, and trims.

For square and rectangular one-piece boxes (those that are purchased flat with tabs and slits for construction), gently pull apart the glued edge of the box. Smooth wet wallpaper on the box; allow to dry overnight. Cut off wallpaper edge around box, and cut slits as on the box itself. Fold on fold lines to construct box. Glue together edges of box that were originally glued. Draw a gold line around the front of the box edge, if desired. Tie with bows and trims.

For pyramid-shaped boxes, wet wallpaper and smooth onto the rough side of the poster board. Allow to dry overnight. Draw a square the desired size on the white side of the poster board. Mark the midpoint of each side of the square. Draw a line perpendicular to the midpoint of each side that extends to the height of the package contents. With a ruler, draw a line from the top of the midpoint line to each end of each side of the square. The overall drawing will resemble a four-pointed star with a square in the center and four identical triangles extending outward from sides *(figure 1)*. Cut out star-shaped figure.

Fold each point up to form a pyramid by using a ruler to create a sharp crease *(figure 2)*. Place figure flat with wallpaper side up, and draw a gold line around the outside edge of the star-shaped figure. Punch a hole in the point of each triangle. Turn figure so that white side faces up, then place contents in tissue on square, then bring up sides and thread ribbon through all holes to tie a bow at the top *(figure 3)*. Add a larger bow or tassel.

Tag gifts in special ways by writing names or monograms on the sides of boxes or on the ribbons with a gold marking pen.

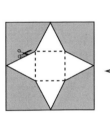

Four-sided pyramid box
(figure 1)

Use ruler to fold up sides into pyramid shape
(figure 2)

Punch holes in each triangle top, and tie with ribbon
(figure 3)

easy does it

CHRISTMAS STOCKING IDEAS

Try these tips for decorating with Christmas stockings:

Use stockings as front door arrangements by tucking in greenery and berries.

Create a unique table arrangement by placing a cylinder with water inside a stocking and filling it with greenery.

Use miniature stockings to hold napkins, silver, name tags, or flowers at individual settings. To make stockings stand upright, insert a small toothpick holder, vase, or cardboard tube.

valentine's *tea* party for children

PEANUT BUTTER AND
HONEY SANDWICHES
ON WHEAT BREAD

STRAWBERRY JAM HEARTS

GINGERBREAD SCONES

STRAWBERRIES, KIWIS,
AND GRAPES

SUGAR MUFFIN
CUPCAKE HEARTS

HEART SUGAR COOKIES

GRAHAM CRACKER
COOKIES

STRAWBERRY CREAM-
FILLED MERINGUES

APPLE JUICE

PEANUT BUTTER AND HONEY SANDWICHES ON WHEAT BREAD

1 small jar creamy peanut butter
1 small jar honey
12 slices wheat bread

Spread a thin layer of peanut butter on each slice of bread. Spread honey on one side of 6 of the slices; top with remaining 6 slices. Cut into heart shapes with cookie cutter. Yield: 6 sandwiches.

Send out **heart-shaped** invitations to little friends. Set up small tables and chairs, and let the children serve themselves.

STRAWBERRY JAM HEARTS

12 slices white bread
1 small jar strawberry jam

Cut bread into heart shapes with cookie cutter. Spread with jam, leaving a small edge all the way around. Yield: 12 open-faced sandwiches.

GINGERBREAD SCONES

2 cups all-purpose flour
3 tablespoons brown sugar
2 teaspoons baking powder
1 teaspoon ground ginger
½ teaspoon baking soda
¼ teaspoon salt
½ teaspoon ground cinnamon
¼ cup cold butter or margarine
⅓ cup molasses
¼ cup milk
1 egg, separated
Sugar

Preheat oven to 400 degrees. In a large bowl, combine first 7 ingredients. Cut in butter or margarine until mixture resembles coarse crumbs. In a small bowl, combine molasses, milk, and egg yolk until smooth; stir into flour mixture just until moistened. Turn out onto floured surface; knead gently 6-8 times. Pat into an 8-inch circle; cut into 12 wedges, and place 1 inch apart on a greased baking sheet. Beat egg white until frothy; brush over scones. Sprinkle with sugar. Bake for 12-15 minutes or until golden brown. Serve warm. Yield: 1 dozen.

Add pink **flowered** braid to napkins and satin bows to the corners of table toppers.

GOLD-LEAF HEART VASES

Create a valentine mood by turning ordinary glass containers into beautiful decorative accessories with a little gold leaf.

You will need:

Clear glass vases and containers of various shapes and sizes, especially hearts
Clear acrylic sealer
Adhesive sizing
Gold leaf sheets
Stencil brush

Paint clear sealer along the edges, in heart shapes on the sides, or on the entire container that is to be gold-leafed. Next, paint with the adhesive sizing, and allow to dry. Carefully spread thin gold leaf sheets on the surface. Smooth with a brush, and seal with more clear sealer. Fill with traditional red or pink roses for the perfect romantic centerpiece.

SUGAR MUFFIN CUPCAKE HEARTS

4 cups all-purpose flour
1 tablespoon baking powder
½ teaspoon salt
2 cups sugar
½ cup butter, melted
2 cups milk
2 eggs
1 tablespoon vanilla extract
1 (16-ounce) can cream cheese frosting

Preheat oven to 400 degrees. Grease bottoms of heart-shaped muffin tins. Sift flour, baking powder, and salt into a large bowl; add sugar. Set aside. Add melted butter to milk, eggs, and vanilla extract. Beat with a fork to mix well. Make a well in the center of flour mixture, and pour in milk mixture all at once. Stir quickly with a fork, just until all ingredients are moistened. Do not beat, or batter will become lumpy. Spoon batter into muffin tins, filling each slightly more than half full. Bake for 15-20 minutes. Frost with canned cream cheese frosting. Yield: 3 dozen.

HEART SUGAR COOKIES

2 cups all-purpose flour
1½ teaspoons baking powder
¼ teaspoon salt
½ cup butter or margarine
1 cup sugar
1 egg
1 tablespoon evaporated milk
1½ teaspoons vanilla

Preheat oven to 375 degrees. Sift flour, baking powder, and salt, and set aside. Cream butter and sugar. Add egg, milk, and vanilla. Add flour mixture. Roll out to about ⅛ to ¼ inch thick, and cut into hearts. Bake for about 15 minutes. Do not overbake. Top with Glaze. Yield: 16-24.

GLAZE:
2 cups confectioner's sugar
¼ stick margarine
¼ cup evaporated milk
½ teaspoon vanilla

Mix together all ingredients. Brush over cookies.

Serve as many **heart-shaped** foods as possible.

Heart-shaped cookies
make wonderful favors.

GRAHAM CRACKER COOKIES

2 cups sugar
½ cup evaporated milk
6 tablespoons butter
20 large marshmallows
2 cups graham cracker crumbs
½ cup flaked coconut
1 cup nuts, chopped

Mix sugar, milk, and butter in a large saucepan. Bring to a boil, and cook for 3 minutes. Add marshmallows, graham cracker crumbs, coconut, and nuts. Drop by teaspoonfuls onto waxed paper, and let cool. Yield: about 2 dozen.

STRAWBERRY CREAM-FILLED MERINGUES

MERINGUES:
2 egg whites
½ cup sugar

Preheat oven to 250 degrees. Line 2 baking sheets with parchment paper. In a bowl, beat egg whites with sugar until soft peaks form. Spoon meringues into a pastry bag fitted with a large star tip. Pipe 24 stars onto prepared baking sheets. Bake for 1 hour or until dry and crisp. Cool on wire racks.

FILLING:
⅔ cup whipping cream
4 medium-size strawberries, hulled
2 teaspoons confectioner's sugar
2 teaspoons water
6 to 8 strawberries, sliced

In a bowl, whip cream until stiff peaks form. In a food processor, process 4 strawberries until smooth. Stir in confectioner's sugar and water. Add to cream, and mix together well. Sandwich meringues together with strawberry cream and sliced strawberries. Yield: 12-16.

Equip a table with **art supplies**
to make valentines to take home.

Children's parties should be **short.**
About 1-1½ hours is probably enough time
for fun for children 10 and under.

TEA CUP CHANDELIER

Add teacups, butterflies, and crystals to a chandelier to create the perfect fixture above your favorite tea table or for a special little lady's bedroom. Simply have tea cups and saucers drilled with holes to fit over the candleholder socket stems. This can be done at any store where glass is cut. Place saucers, then cups, on each candle arm, then replace candleholder covers. Add butterflies or other decorations with glue, and attach crystals and crystal chains.

index

Recipe Index

Easy Does It Project Index

Recipe Credits

Elaine Atkins
Blackberry Jam, Christmas Punch, Pumpkin Bread with Sweet Cream Spread, Pumpkin Parfait

Sarabeth Atkins
Almond Eggnog Baby Bundt Cakes, Apple-Cinnamon Sandwiches, Striped Ham Sandwiches

Candy Blue
Italian Cream Cake

Kelli Bozeman
Applesauce Spice Cake with Candied Pecans

Corinne Bradford
Yellow Squash Stuffed with Spinach

Lena Causey
Artichoke Soup, Baked Turkey Sandwiches on Cinnamon-Raisin Bread, Crab Cakes with Caper Sauce, Grilled Vegetables with Toasted Sesame Seeds, Herb Cheese Biscuits, Lemon Icebox Cake, Sesame Biscuits, Steak Fajitas, Yellow Cake with Easy Caramel Icing

Peggy Causey
Wild Rice Toss

Vera Everett
Blueberry Cobbler, Italian Broiled Tomatoes

Peggy Foggin
Raspberry or Strawberry Jam

Pam Glover
Sesame Asparagus Roll-ups

Gale Hammond
Crispy Broccoli Salad, Pecan Pie Muffins, Strawberry Pecan Cake

Linn Harris
Chicken Chow Mein, Fruit Tea, Hot Peach Casserole

Rosie Henderson
Cheese Grits

Anna Henson
Easy Tiramisu

Lynn Hill
Bell Peppers Stuffed with Corn Salad

Madalyn Hindman
Cream Cheese Tarts with Cherries

Carolyn Hodges
Berry Spritzer

Linda Hogue
Brunch Casserole

Katy Houston
Baked Chili Relleños, Cheddar Cheese Biscuits with Ham, Honey-Yogurt Sauce on Fruit, Pumpkin Muffins with Orange Pecan Butter, Raspberry Cream Cheese Coffee Cake

Joyce Jones
Gingerbread Scones, Peaches and Cream Cake

Maggi Lampton
Flower Cupcakes

Mayme Lukey
Spicy Tomato Aspic

Mildred McCorstin
Butter Crisp Cookies

Mary Jane McDaniel
Fresh Fruit Bowl with Spiced Fruit Dressing, Grilled Pork Tenderloin

Emily Moore
Mimi's Kahlua Brownies

Sally Randall
Pumpkin Pie Cake

Linda Rochelle
Berries in a Cloud

Pat Ross
Beaten Biscuits, Classic Butterscotch Pie, Pork Medallions with Mustard Cream Sauce, Spinach Roulade, Spicy Tomato Soup, Sweet Potato Molds with Cranberry Sauce

Mrs. J.E. (Mary) Sherrod
Tiny Orange Muffins with Cranberry Chutney and Turkey

Evelyn Slay
Beef Roast, Potatoes, and Carrots; Butterscotch Delight; Caramel Squares; Graham Cracker Cookies; Heart Sugar Cookies; Homemade Vanilla Ice Cream

Mary Elizabeth Waggoner
Lemon Tart Filling

Charla Walker
Easy Chocolate Icing

Marian Ware
Citrus Fruit Cups with Orange-Mint Dressing

Susan Wellington
Butter Sugar Cookies

Easy Does It Project Credits

Judy Davis
Gingerbread Spice Ornaments

Charlotte Kidd
Fruit and Vegetable Turkey

Mary Jane McDaniel
Moss Bunny

Elizabeth Pegg
Posy Bags

Photography Credits

Greg Campbell
Pages 2, 6-10, 12-14, 16, 17, 19, 20 (upper right), 21 (upper two photos), 22, 23 (left), 26-34, 36, 37, 38 (right), 42, 43, 45-47, 50, 51, 53, 54, 56, 57 (bottom), 59-62, 63 (top), 64, 66-72, 74-82, 84-91, 93-101; back cover (upper right, lower two photos)

David Johnston
Dust jacket back flap

Tempy Segrest
Front cover; pages 3, 4, 11, 18, 20 (lower left), 21 (lower left), 23 (right), 24, 25, 38 (left), 39-41, 44, 48, 49, 52, 55, 57 (upper left), 58, 63 (lower three photos), 102, and 103; back cover (upper left)